Garden
Ornaments

AREND JAN VAN DER HORST

INTRODUCTION BY RICHARD ROSENFELD

REBO
PRODUCTIONS

© 1995 Zuid Boekprodukties, Lisse

© 1996 Published by Rebo Productions Ltd

Text: *Arend Jan van der Horst*

Cover design: *Ton Wienbelt, The Netherlands*

Photo editing: *TextCase, The Netherlands*

Production: *TextCase, The Netherlands*

Translation: *Suzanne Walters for First Edition Translations Ltd, Great Britain*

Typesetting: *Fairfield Systems for First Edition Translations Ltd, Great Britain*

Photograph centre front cover: © *A. Beysens,*

1995 c/o Beeldrecht Amsterdam

Contents

ISBN 1

Foreword

You can always tell a good garden, not by its flamboyant effects, roses piled on roses, and outrageous 200ft long borders, but by the tiniest, significant detail. The way the paths are made up, how the lawn is edged, the wood that is used for the trellis, the ways of dividing space. These are the ideas that count.

I like the way Arend Jan van der Horst tackles subjects like garden lighting. He comes straight out with it - "I do not really like these nostalgic lamps" ("these" being the old street lamps you can buy, not that cheaply, in reclamation yards all over the country). What is his alternative? Modern, Danish aluminium lamps and "bull's-eye", storm lamps, mounted on a square wooden post. This is a book with ideas.

I got my first lesson in the importance of style, visiting a secretly tucked away garden in a stone-built, very posh village where Oxfordshire becomes the Cotswolds, and the Range Rovers are just a bit smarter. Up the lane from the church there's this foliage-packed, architectural garden in the most impeccable taste, created not by one but eight people. An Oxford don and his ex-students.

They had assembled all kinds of elements, and you never spotted the join. A hint of the 18th century when you would take a fixed route round the garden, interpreting the statues and historical allusions, seeing your place in the general scheme of things. There's a Greek temple with a quote from Blake inscribed, and the gentle ding of windchimes. There are rustic, Gothic seats, and modern tables and chairs. A clean-cut pond shaped like a cross, an Edwardian parterre decorated with fuchsias and tulips in gravel, and a magnificent king-size urn. But best of all there is a garden lampstand, made by Vico Magistretti in the early 20th century, with tight metal loops and flourishes.

Everywhere you looked the artificial had a natural twin. Fibreglass lions and topiarised birds, vertical wooden shapes (a pergola), and a standard (Robinia hispida). Big chunky balls of box, and

olive pots. I even saw a Versaille pot with a lush green *Musa* banana tree. No-one ever bothers with lawn edging, but here they'd hemmed it in with black metal strips. It tidies everything up.

Steps are too often ignored but Arend Jan van der Horst takes you through the alternatives. Grey paving stones, concrete steps, U-shape concrete blocks (also good for walls), or iroko wood from Africa. I also like the way he virtually gets down on his hands and knees, and gives us the low-down on gardens, showing us what he has designed. The millstone fountain at the Mien Ruys Water Foundation, with water running out of an attractive old stone. And even how plants can be used as ornaments.

This might sound like sacrilege but some plants have shape, others don't, and it's silly not to see their potential. For grey mobile planting try *Elaeagnus ebbingei*. A dense, bushy evergreen, growing 5m (15ft) high. It has marvelous glossy green leaves, with a silvery-grey hue beneath. It's invaluable in the border, but have you ever tried highlighting it in a pot? Topiarised like a square or a ball? Or tried mixing *Artemisia* with scented *Heliotropium*?

Perfecting a new garden takes time. You can always have a go yourself, but it's so much better with a wink and a nod from someone who has done it before. Someone to point out the pitfalls. To give you the right advice. The only problem with this excellent book is, if you've already finished your garden, it makes you want to start all over gain.

Garden furnishings, pots, and parasols

If you are thinking of buying new garden furniture, you would do well to decide first on the ambience which the garden as a whole is to convey.

Do you want to create a place outdoors where everything is designed for sitting outside in the greatest of comfort, sunbathing and entertaining friends? Or is your garden supposed to convey the idea of a paradise of wild plants?

To help unsuspecting buyers in their choice I will give a few examples of what can look right and what can look totally wrong. The main consideration is the important role that the type of garden furniture plays in creating the ambience.

Garden owners for the most part want white garden furniture which is comfortable to sit in and easy to clean. I should think this can be seen in 90 per cent of gardens. The requirement of a comfortable seat is understandable, for what is more delightful than to be able to eat, drink coffee, and sunbathe in a chair all day without being troubled by back pain? This is a great advantage of furniture which is made mainly of synthetic materials and is also the reason that you see so much of it nowadays.

With a lot of other garden furniture made of wood, iron, and even concrete, the less time you spend on it the better. I often think that most of this kind of furniture is too conspicuous, especially bearing in mind that the plants in the garden deserve to have first claim on the attention. That is why I want to examine the various ways of integrating colour with environment, even with a set of white garden furniture.

It is easy to linger at table in this classic French terrace armchair. The colour scheme is restrained, black with grey.

5

White flowers with a set of white furniture

Grey and white are in plentiful supply in the choice of garden plants these days. There are white roses, for example, with *Rosa* 'Schnee-wittchen', which blooms from June to October, as the front runner. The grey leaf of *Stachys*, *Artemesia* and *Naphalis* gives a refined effect during this time of year to the white flowers and green leaf forms. I once designed a garden for a modern house, the interior of which gave emphasis to black and white. A black sofa and large white tiles on the floor made the interior a strong and decorative entity. The house itself was built like a box with few fascinating basic features which could be repeated in the garden. At best, the straight angles of the façade, which in fact were attractively staggered, were able to offer a starting point. So I chose a number of black-stained wooden platforms. Since then, my advice for this sort of wooden floor, which is constantly being walked on, has been to stain it three times with an outdoor stain. Above these platforms I put a pergola with posts which repeated the rhythm of the window frames. The terraces were square and I allowed their levels to be staggered in such a way that it was possible to step from one platform to the next. This is handy, because all areas can then be reached equally easily. One terrace had a pergola with a reinforced glass roof, under which could stand the set of white furniture which the owners already had. Grey and white striped cushions were added and next to them white troughs of white marguerite daisies. In this way good integration of

This classic dark-painted garden bench fits perfectly into its background: a feathered, black-stained barn in a Brabant garden.

black and white was achieved outside too, and was most effective.
If you look carefully you will discover that not all white furniture necessarily has to be made of synthetic material. You also come across cane and iron used for seating. The idea of matching the planting to the furniture as regards colour is still important, however.

The colour of these pieces of furniture, which achieve an air of sculptures, is known as Swedish or peasant blue.

White furniture with a delicate border of perennials

One of the most beautiful gardens in the Netherlands is next to a white house. White garden furniture stands on the spacious lawn which is situated behind the living-room. Behind this furniture is the border, which has been recorded in numerous photographs in books and magazines. There are a great many grey tints in this semicircular strip planted with green-leafed perennials. There are carnations, *Dianthus*, *Artemesias*, and the grey-leafed *Lysimachia ephemerum*, which grows as a climber and is white-flowering with a profusion of small flowers. The large amount of grey among the plants with their blue, pink, and white flowers is extremely effective.

The white of the house is taken up in the border by the white flowers and grey leaf colours, and the white garden furniture is used for the same purpose; it forms a transition from the house to the green lawn and the border of perennials. The furniture is made of white-painted cane, which is delightful to sit in and easily moved. With this simple furniture I have never had the urge to move it to a far corner of the garden, as I soon have with synthetic furniture.

Colourful flowers as a diversion tactic

I once stepped into the garden of the Hoge Heerlijkheid restaurant in Middelharnis, in the Netherlands. The garden was strangely divided up. Along one side raised plant borders and plant troughs of vertical wood had been fixed, in which there was a colourful assortment of annuals almost at table height. By drawing the plant troughs into the shape of half-arches round each little terrace and by continually repeating this along the side, niches were created in which each dining table acquired its own intimacy. The eye was drawn towards them by the colourful plants in the troughs and no one took any further notice of the furniture placed there. This idea proves successful, provided that the colour scheme is tastefully arranged. For people who have trouble bending, it is a good idea to raise the plant borders. At the restaurant it was lovely for the guests to sit in a flower border which was the same height as the table.

I once saw the most beautifully filled terracotta pots in the most unexpected place: outside a building at a university.

White furniture with abundantly filled pots

There they stood: large terracotta pots with festoons, in which a colourful mixture of annuals had developed into a fanciful world of tall, short and trailing flowers. There were white annual marguerite daisies, light blue lobelia, pink trailing geraniums, with yellow *Calceolaria*, or slipperwort, incorporated into them, together with grey *Helichrysum*. Tall *Araceana* stood in a tuft in the middle, and

White iron furniture is often covered with wooden parts to make the seats feel more comfortable. Here is a splendid combination on a terrace of small yellow bricks.

because they were the standard variety they lent a stately air to the fanciful swirling mass. Light-tinted fuchsias hung between the annuals. *Verbena patagonica*, the tall slender purple-blooming verbena, provided the necessary height.

If you have a large terrace you can plant a series of identical pots each year with tall, middle-sized or short trailing plants in a wide range of delicate and bright colours. The plants needed to provide height, standard fuchsias, tall, standard dracaenas and standard marguerites, can be a problem. You have to buy new ones each year, which is expensive, or keep an eye on them in the greenhouse or the house. This is possible, provided that the room is light and not too warm, preferably even cold. A garage with a window or a barn which you can keep the frost out of is also suitable. Place the pots in a row or round the table and the white chairs and you will be surrounded by overwhelming luxury. Fertilize regularly for long, abundant flowering, as the fertilizers which you put into the pot with the earth are quickly used up.

A combination of eighteenth-century garden ornaments. Give white benches and ornaments a solid background of hedging or bush conifers such as yew to soften the white, otherwise it can easily dominate.

Leaf shapes around a white bistro table and chairs

Some hostas have such striking leaves that the whole of our attention is drawn to them. *Hosta sieboldiana* 'Frances Williams', for example, has that effect. The leaves appear to have a blue film, a quite definite blue, and have a yellow edge. This combination of blue and yellow is hardly ever found naturally in leaves, not even in the varieties obtained from nurseries.

A 'Frances Williams' in a pot

The side sections of this bench are loosely fitted because the boards sometimes rot. Make sure you use rounded board sections with elegant wrought-iron sides like these.

Although I could see no white garden furniture near it, a florist convinced me of the beauty of this hosta. He had planted overhead plants on a patio to soften the light. In this half-shadow stood at least twelve identical terracotta pots with only the 'Frances Williams' in them. The leaves were large and it was a magnificent sight, because of the harmony which had been applied to the planting of the pots. For some time I had already been putting pots with green hosta or the blue *Hosta sieboldiana-elegans* on the terraces I had designed, next to globes of box and pots of trailing ivy. The tranquillity enables you to experience the entirety, rather than looking at individual pots which have been scattered around as disconnected ornamentation.

Anyone who has been to France will regard the French bistro chairs as integral with that country. Though the term bistro chair refers to a group of garden furniture, the word does not tell us much about the model. It should not be assumed that this is a case of the very simplest shape, with a straight back and a seat consisting of straight or, more accurately, slightly bent slats. A white round, straight or rectangular bistro table goes with them, and possibly also a white parasol. Place this on a platform, a flagstone terrace, or on gravel or grass and just put hostas in pots beside it, preferably all in the same colour.

Once you have seen this you will no longer need bright colours, but you will choose harmony and simplicity. The green-leafed *Hosta undulata* has white flowers. If you have a spot for a splendid combi-

It could hardly be more idyllic in this large, silent space where it is so pleasant to sit in the shade.

nation like this put in some *Hosta fortunei* 'Hyacintha' as well, which has fresh green elongated leaves with lance-shaped veins.

White plastic wire chairs

It was supposedly an Italian who thought of the idea of winding plastic wire, which was strong enough to sit or lie on, round a framework of aluminium. And these plastic wire chairs are actually wonderful for sitting in. Problems arise when the wire breaks, as they are difficult to mend. The only solution, in fact, is to have all the wire renewed. Wire chairs have the attractive quality of combining well with other garden furniture. On my terrace I would place modern troughs next to them, painted dun-coloured for instance. But you can also have simple square concrete troughs with them, or black-painted wooden troughs. For the troughs I would use one colour as the basis and put only one sort of plant in them at a time.

Blue heliotrope is splendid for the summer and in the winter I would put blue violets in them. Blue lobelia with globes or squares of box seems to me a splendid combination of delicate and sturdy. Very tall white cleome is equally beautiful or the greeny-yellow of the tall slender tobacco plant *Nicotiana langsdorfii*. In short, it is a delight to invent your own white large or small pots and troughs or to choose plants for the garden to go with garden furniture, which integrate with white, to create a special harmony.

This particular corner bench can be left outside.

Furniture to catch the eye: wooden and iron benches

A bench can be an outstanding focal point in a garden or part of the garden, as it is not possible to put statues and pots everywhere.

A bench, in my opinion, is the simplest form of large ornament. For it should not be forgotten that most benches are wide, have a back, and a characteristic shape. The amazing thing is that the English garden bench has had such a boom.

This sturdy bench stands in front of a wall of natural stone, on a path which is also made of natural stone. The ivy is mature, the cherry blossom delicate.

English teak garden benches

Everyone knows the English parks with their tranquil rustic benches, most of them wide with backs and arms. England with its many colonies was the first to consider the use of hardwood garden ornaments and in so doing started off a real craze.

The Dutch were not familiar with the use of teak for garden furniture, apart from the chairs on the decks of ships travelling to the Far East. These so-called deckchairs are dealt with separately.

Teak benches have stood for years in English parks, in spots where people can sit under a tree in the shade. They stand in places where you can catch the first spring sunshine without sitting in a draught, where you can watch the pigeons being fed, near ponds, in children's playgrounds and in rose gardens; you even see them awaiting passengers in train stations.

They became so popular with regular visitors to parks that many made gifts of a bench to the community park management and then asked if they could add a copper plate bearing their name. A clever idea, which other countries should also emulate; their parks would then look a lot more attractive. It would certainly be a success, having a

bench as a personal gift. Maybe everyone should start in their own local park.

Besides the straight models, there are differently-shaped benches which curve inwards and which enable people to talk to each other. Because this is of course the drawback of a straight bench: sitting next to each other and having to turn your head to be able to communicate can become a nuisance after a while. If three people want to converse it is completely impossible. Hence the corner bench or round bench.

The huge Gunnera *leaf overhangs this elegant wood structure, which shows that you can successfully combine the simple with the baroque (Giardini in Kalmthout, Belgium).*

Semicircular benches at Hever Castle

If you have a large garden you will know the problem of lack of intimacy. One solution can be to create a separate corner, or even, in very large gardens, an entire garden enclosed by bushes, hedges, or in some other way (for example by trellises).

I have seen this done to good effect in the large garden of Hever Castle, Kent, the castle where Anne Boleyn was born and grew up. This second wife of Henry VIII lived in a small castle, which was built of brick and enclosed by a moat, during the transition from the Middle Ages to the Renaissance. At that time the men wore hats like berets and short, wide knickerbockers, the women long gowns and white caps. Their gardens consisted of leafy avenues of pear or beech trees and flower gardens in complicated mathematical patterns with all sorts of topiary in them. There were mazes and orchards with wild flowers.

This atmosphere was restored by Lord Astor who bought Hever Castle at the beginning of this century. He built an extension to the castle, widened the moat, and created a new maze and several formal gardens with yew hedges.

Italian nymphs can sit in the dry on this ornamental bench.

Apart from this historical layout a large new garden was constructed. This was because Lord Astor was an avid collector of Roman and Greek statues, sarcophagi, pillars and anything made of marble or freestone in ancient times in the way of an ornament. When he was ambassador for England in Italy he had collected enthusiastically and knew how to get his collection out of the country. But where was he to put all those stone ladies and gentlemen, those pillars and marble fragments? The solution: two avenues were laid out to the left and right of an expansive lawn which led in a straight line to an enormous pond-cum-lake. The two paths were roofed with pergolas. The pergolas were supported on freestone pillars and were completely overgrown with blue wisteria and other decorative climbing plants. On one side of the paths walls were built, so that the whole thing – the middle of the lawn and the two paths to the left and right – was enclosed. Between the paths and the wall a small strip was inserted to create spaces for the statues and ornaments. These are separated from each other by conifers and bushes. Every lover of ornaments ought to see this fascinating tableau at least once. It shows us that collecting has consequences if the objects are to be well displayed.

The foot of this bench is lyre-shaped, to create an elegant impression of being old. The material is freestone which can take on a greenish appearance in time. The speed with which this happens depends on the pores; if they are open, attack is fast. If the surface is smooth, the process takes place more slowly.

Whilst a layout like this is, of course, very nice, and even very impressive, it is not exactly the most inviting or cosy place to sit for a while out of the wind. This is why the large middle lawn, broken up by a sunken conservatory, is enclosed all round by yew hedges. Depth is created by building little walls round the dug-out patch of lawn. These boundary walls of sandstone give a colourful, now rather mossy effect. Flower borders have been put in between the walls and the surrounding yew hedges, so that there is something to look at.

The semicircular teak benches have been placed here inside semicircular brick walls, so that people can stop during the walk along the row of statues and talk to each other.

There is plenty to recount about the history of this unique collection, which also includes a secret section which only scholars are allowed to see. These contain the rather scabrous depictions of lovers from antiquity. The need to depict carnal love already existed at that time.

There is no wind in the sunken garden, which can be wonderful. There is often full sun and there are flowers and a tranquil evergreen hedge to look at. And then of course there are the semicircular teak benches, which have a beauty of their own.

A teak corner bench in the garden of Garden Gallery

An advantage of this garden in Eext, in the Netherlands, is that you see the furniture in a splendid garden situation, so that you can judge the scale and the effect of this for the most part rather substantial

This wrought-iron bench is old and fortunately has not yet been copied. A valuable eye-catcher, it is painted pale grey-blue.

furniture, if you are thinking about putting something similar in your own garden. In one of the gardens which I designed for the two owners a border of poisonous plants has been put in. This sounds sinister, but is not really. There are a lot of plants which can just as well be called medicinal as poisonous, for small quantities of the poison are used as antidotes to generate antibodies in the human body to attack whatever disease you have.

A "poison border" sounds fascinating and not only that: it is a true spectacle of colour and shape, with some simple plants, such as monkshood, and, in contrast, edible plants, such as the perennial artichoke. What that is doing there, apart from looking good, several feet tall with a mass of silver-grey leaves, I do not know, but there must be an explanation for it.

The interesting thing here is two terraces with teak corner benches, which are on the shady side of this elongated north-south lying garden. I still well remember how I designed the two poison borders which lie opposite each other.

My clients made one alteration to my plan. Grass was sown in the middle of the shady border to give the whole thing some symmetry. At the start of this garden there are borders on both sides to the left and right of the central grass path. These end on both sides, at the start and at the finish, with a square clinker terrace. I designed this as the endpoint so that one could sit here, and one reason for doing so was

Here I made a little swamp the focal point of a long clinker path. On the path stands a simple hardwood bench which looks rather rustic. It is wonderful to be able to gaze at dragonflies and pigeons drinking and to feel oneself alone but not abandoned.

to bring an end to the borders. Corner benches were placed on these terraces, which I had never before seen used in the Netherlands.

It is an ideal spot for talking, possibly in a group of six or eight people, as the benches are big enough for up to four people each side. You could devise a plan for making a love potion . . . or a witch's brew, as a lot of the poison plants were used for these: the unsuspecting drinker was put into a hazy state of mind; he hallucinated and thought he was experiencing wild adventures. Drugs are not something which we have just discovered. This is why a lot of herbalists were burned at the stake as witches.

Teak chairs are always decorative, as can be seen in the garden of Bardsly House.

Iron benches as eye-catchers

Many kinds of very serviceable iron benches are available at the moment, which can be used as eye-catchers. Whether they are always comfortable to sit in is another question. There are various types connected with certain countries. For instance, there is the English iron bench, which has simple horizontal lines for the back and the seat and is usually painted white. I have never come across this model in the Netherlands or Belgium. Possibly it is thought to be too plain.

Then there is the American model, the back lines of which are curved. The sides of the back are straight, and the top goes slightly into the shape of a point and then curves in a half-circle just past the middle of the back. This happens on both the left and the right, resulting in two points with the two lines running across each other in the middle, which leave an oval opening. These benches are often painted mauve-blue. There are matching chairs so that you can have a set of table and chairs. They are also good as the endpoint of a small avenue, especially in small-scale situations, because the benches are very transparent and therefore do not appear to take up much room. This has come about by using plated steel, which is fortunately galvanized, so there is no need to worry about rust. The original American benches are recognizable from the ridges in the plated steel at the front.

Once I saw a strange application of one of these in a vegetable garden. The owner of the garden planted two beds to the left and right of a field of red cabbage. A small bench in exactly the same purpley-mauve colour stood behind them as the endpoint of the blue plants. The result was a mini-spectacle.

If you like orange East Indian cherries, you should paint the bench deep orange, in an avenue of lady's mantle it should be yellow-ochre, and with red flower borders crimson.

However, it is usually the bluey-grey and greeny-grey colours which first come to mind when choosing a colour for these simple benches.

The fount of inspiration
At the time of the migration to America some European Baptists settled in that land of promise. Whole regions of Europe were depopulated by this wave of emigration. The Baptists called themselves

I divided up this long narrow space with hedges, perennials, ornamental grass, and a statue by André Volten, and I used two identical benches to link them together.

Methodists in America, or Mennonites, after their minister, the Reverend Menno Simons. They lived in a monk-like fashion, without marrying, the men separate from the women. They made a lot of furniture for their own buildings and this furniture has acquired the name of "Shaker furniture". "Shaker" derives from the rhythmic dance which the believers performed at their religious services. The Mennonites used Dutch colours from the sixteenth and seventeenth centuries to paint their furniture: ox-blood red, pale blue, dull greyish green, bluey green, grey and yellow ochre. These colours can often be seen in Dutch farms and mansions from that period. Their furniture is a classic example of the theory that "less is more" and it seems to work with them. The benches, chairs, and tables have become museum pieces. Fortunately they are being brought onto the market again, though they are very expensive. The American wrought-iron bench fits into this tradition of less is more. The result, alas, is that one cannot sit on them for long. They are therefore pre-eminently suitable for teashops, which want to achieve a high turnover of their tea and coffee drinkers. They can be used to perch on in the garden, preferably with a cushion, as they are certainly very hard to sit on.

Curved scrolls as a basic shape

Some English benches, mostly white-painted, have round lines as their basic shape. The benches are comfortable to sit on, as you can sit on them for some time without feeling the ridges on the seat and the

A number of pretty garden ornaments have been given their own spot in this romantic flower garden. In early spring the white bench, which has just been brought outside again, attracts all the attention. This is not surprising, as there are not many flowers to admire yet.

back. The back and seat consist of horizontal iron bands, with round lines which curl inwards as foot and back supports; the iron can be painted or left as it is. This attractive, elegant type of bench is suited to a rather formal setting.

I once put a bench like this next to a large wrought-iron summer-house in the sculpture garden at Heeswijk-Dinther. The summer-house is straight and rigid and was soon overgrown with white wisteria. The bench with its round lines stood a little way away and made a good contrast. This is a good choice with a straight fence, a straight pond, a rigidly-cut hedge, or an avenue of fruit trees. Make sure you can look at it from the opposite side by making a diagonal link with the terrace on which the round bench stands. Then you can see the curves nicely and its beauty is visible.

I shall return to iron furniture in a later chapter, when I shall show how wooden boards soon started to be mounted on the iron frame, because iron is so difficult to sit on. Wood is warm and more comfortable to sit on, while iron is cold and soon becomes uncomfortable because of the bands used to cover the back and seat surfaces.

Some garden furniture uses boards into which holes are punched. The water can then drain away when it rains. This is a good solution to seating problems, which is why you see this system used so much for all sorts of terrace furniture. In particular, French bistro and park chairs are made in these materials. Fortunately new ones are being

To create space the grass has been brought as close as possible to the bench. The stone is there to keep the feet dry.

Garden furniture in the garden of a farm

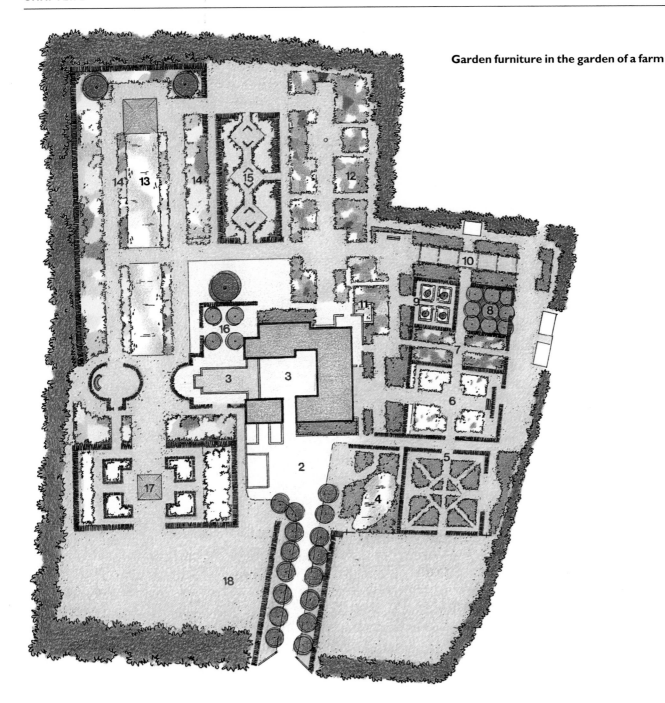

1 a small path with bays, a hedge and mossy pillars, and beyond, the long lime avenue

2 gravel front square

3 inner square with a large, new, blue glasshouse

4 pond with *Gunnera* and other large swamp plants

5 kitchen garden

6 white garden

7 kitchen garden with ferns, Christmas roses and *Euphorbia*

8 ivy patch with fruit bushes

9 herb garden with central ornament

10 large arches for climbing roses, framed by large coltsfoot

11 small pond beside terraces and purple, lilac and blue plants; the large borders continue this theme and are planted in the same colours

12 in the middle of the small circle is an ornamental vase of Haddonstone on a plinth

13 long pond with a boggy area in the middle and a summer-house at the end

14 yellow and grey plants of *Pyrus salicifolia*

15 bamboo garden for displaying ornaments

16 half-paving of dolomite (boulder clay) for displaying garden furniture, with low beech hedge and overhead plane trees

17 section not yet laid out

18 parking area

This classical arrangement looks a little bizarre with the high hedges, but it is certainly impressive. Taxus baccata has been chosen for the hedge. The bench looks rather puny because of the high walls, but the statues are still well in proportion.

Just right for a bench: tiles in front of it keep the feet dry and warm. This green bench would also be a modest, but attractive, eye-catcher in a small garden.

produced. This is often slender furniture with thin backs and arms, but with punched-out back and seat surfaces, so that sitting becomes a true pleasure. To maintain the transparency, the backs are often made simply of round iron rods, which look attractive, but are less comfortable for sitting.

Bear in mind that iron rusts, so you must put some sort of cover on iron furniture which will not leave marks on light-coloured clothes. You often see this in France: men put their newspapers on the terrace chairs in the park before they sit on them. A cushion is undoubtedly a much more comfortable solution if you insist on furniture which will rust when exposed to the weather.

It is better, of course, to check whether new chairs made in old styles are galvanized. They are naturally rather more expensive to buy, but far more practical, because there is no risk of rust. Painting is also kept to a minimum.

Rust is the great disadvantage of antique benches, chairs and tables. Because of the construction of the flat bands which lie on top of each other you cannot reach all the rust spots. If this furniture always stands outside an annual scraping and painting session is recommended. That is why many people bring this furniture into the house and use it as conservatory, breakfast, or dining-room chairs instead. There it is just as effective as when it is used outside.

I am myself a great lover of antique garden furniture and I have such tables and chairs in my home wherever possible.

There is a lot of choice in benches and nearly all models are reproduced. So take care if you buy an antique iron bench from a street-seller who is not known to be *bona fide*. If a new bench has rusted you cannot always tell the difference between a bench that was made last week and one has stood in a French provincial town since it was first placed there a hundred years ago.

I have myself caught *bona fide* traders selling new furniture as old. But if you have not paid too much you can forget the origin and enjoy the splendid slender shapes of this eye-catching iron furniture in the garden.

From deckchair to wall seat

What is more delightful than finding a spot from time to time where you can lie stretched out, whether in the sun or not? On a hot day it is just as pleasant in the shade of a tree as it is in the warmth of the sun on a rather cooler day. There are lots of different ways of catching the sun.

The sort of reclining chairs created by our grandparents were not so silly as we sometimes think. They were the first people to go on long voyages on ships *en route* to the colonies or to go on lengthy cruises. In good weather they went out on deck, not so much to sit in the sun, because they certainly were not interested in getting a suntan. No, they preferred to sit under awnings in a cool breeze in a comfortable chair, where they could doze, read, or chat to a partner or fellow passenger.

It was soon discovered that it is very relaxing to be able to rest your legs on a little footrest. If you are familiar with boats, you will know that it can be very calm, but it can also be very rough in storms or a swell. There was therefore a need for furniture which was sturdy and which could stand outside day and night. Thus arose the famous deckchairs, which were originally placed in long rows on the "decks" of the ships.

They were made of wood from the colonies; of hardwood, usually teak. Teak comes from India, Burma, Indonesia and Sri Lanka. It is a slow-growing wood of solid texture, which develops into such a hard wood that teak is also given the name tropical hardwood. And rightly so, for it certainly is hard, as you can tell if you ever have to drive a nail into it. It is almost impossible, so a drill or screws are normally used for putting together anything in this sort of wood. Another characteristic of hardwood is that it never, or hardly ever,

Deckchairs are made of hardwood, so they can stay outside and go grey like sculptures amongst the greenery.

rots. It seems to go on for ever, although there certainly is a limit to the time before it starts to weather. This wood goes grey if it stands outside. On the ship's deck the wood was probably dipped in oil, because people at that time thought that wood which had gone grey looked rather shabby.

Since not everyone wanted to sit with their feet up all the time, the footrests were made so that they could be taken away or folded underneath. Cushions, which were specially made for the purpose, were put on the chairs and travelling rugs helped to shield the delicate ladies *and* the delicate gentlemen from the cold of the sometimes over-fresh sea wind.

Contoured boards are normally used for platforms to prevent them becoming slippery. Here the boards are flat and laid in squares in different directions, in order to break up the length and create terraces.

The deckchair is re-discovered

Four or five years ago the deckchair was re-discovered for the garden, to the great pleasure of many sun-worshippers, although, quite honestly, it is far from ideal for this. After all, you can only sit or lie on your back in these splendid chairs, so your front gets brown, but you still need to buy other furniture in order to tan the back of your body. But lounging is not necessarily the same as sunbathing. If, for instance, you want to read for a while, you have the ideal chair for lounging in, and this also applies if you simply want to have a snooze. The wide arms are good supports and the footrest is ideal. You can often adjust the back to upright, half-upright, and reclining positions. Today's designs with copper fretwork are extremely pretty.

You can leave them outside to go grey, apart from the copper ones, because they become dull.

The chairs have the effect of sculptures in the garden, under a tree, a pergola, on a platform, beside a pond, in the rose garden. In general these are attractive shapes which are nice to see standing around, even when they are not in use.

In this pond garden you can see how platforms can be used as a fanciful link between the house, the pond, and the rest of the garden.

In a garden in Limburg in Belgium I came across a large pond which was enclosed by freestone rims. I was asked to integrate with it a new piece of garden lying next to it, which was approximately 150cm (4ft 6in) lower than the existing pond and the garden. I did it by designing a so-called cascade. A cascade in landscape gardening is a water stairway. The cascade linked the existing pond to a large rectangular area of water on the lower level. Water basins were used as the link: in effect these are small ponds with levels in between. The freestone rims were designed to act as waterfalls.

The water from the lowest pond was pumped to the highest pond, so there was a constant flow and the waterfalls situated one behind the other worked well.

In the lower garden, right behind the sight-line of the waterfalls, I put a slightly sunken terrace to add intimacy and to give the feeling that you could touch the water with your hands while sitting down. In this way there is very direct contact, both physically and visually, between the person who is sitting on the terrace and the water.

I placed deckchairs on the sunken oak terrace and I also had round tables with low legs specially made and placed them among the chairs because, as you become aware when you sit in deckchairs, it is difficult to get up out of them, for instance to take a cup of coffee or a glass of wine from a central table. You actually have to stand up. Also, the arms of the deckchairs are quite high, so it is not easy to pick up a cup of coffee or a glass with a drink in it from the reclining position. Hence my little tables on the same level as the arms of the deckchairs.

There are lots of pots standing by these chairs, which function as sculptures. These deliberately did not contain flowers; there are plenty of those in the rest of the garden.

At my request there are only pots with large green globes of box and spirals of ivy, which are trained into that shape. This creates tranquillity and all the attention is drawn primarily to the pond and after that to the deckchairs with the pots round them.

The Garden Gallery in Eext has two seats opposite the long poison border. Globes of yew have been placed to the left and right of the grass path as support and to give the benches a balance in green.

Cane reclining chairs from grandmother's days

If you look at many French magazines on interiors and gardens you will often see cane reclining chairs with high, straight adjustable backs. The top is straight, the arms are wide and generous, and there is a high footrest to go with the chair. These chairs are obviously being reproduced by enterprising manufacturers, because they are

seen far too often in fine rustic interiors for them all to have origi-
nated from grandmother's days.

Because the cane is quite springy, it is wonderful to sit in. Owing to
its high, long back it is a pleasure for tall people, who can rest their
heads in all positions. Behind the back there is a round stick which
can be adjusted so that you can sit in a reclining position or just a
bit more upright. The footrest is long, and therefore suitable for all
leg lengths.

In short, this is an ideal chair for the conservatory or the built-on
roofed dining terrace, as cane cannot be left outside for too long,
because it eventually decays. However, it decays only after a really
long time, since a slightly damp environment is in fact good for its
durability. An exceptionally dry room is rather inclined to dry out
the cane, in which case it can crack.

You do not have to have cushions, though I usually put a long,
specially made cushion fastened with a string in deckchairs, so it is
possible to sit really comfortably. You can get these cushions in
white, grey and white, dark green and dark Burgundy red. If you are
practical you will choose dark green, if you like a Mediterranean
atmosphere then it will be white, if you have Burgundy red roses in
your garden then your choice will be Burgundy, and if you like pale
colours you will choose ecru with grey.

In the French magazines you normally see these cane reclining

*For a modern house I
designed modern
garden items, such as
bright yellow chairs, a
long, narrow pond
with reed mace and a
black platform, to
bring the rather boring
patio to life.*

armchairs in a conservatory or simply in the living room. You even see them in generously proportioned bathrooms.

Modern wooden reclining chairs

The deckchair is no good if you want a brown back or want to sleep or read on your stomach in the shade. You must be able to put a sunbed flat or, if need be, raise the back slightly. Many people do not know that such a thing already exists: flat hardwood beds on square feet are available, the backs of which can be set at different levels. These sturdy beds make splendid reclining furniture because they do not need any attention. They go grey and become part of the undergrowth and the background. In the summer you can also put a mattress or cushions on them.

Mattresses often have a sort of plasticized cover, so that they can be left outside in the rain. You need to lay on them on a towel so as not to feel the cover which gets hot in the sun.

Walls for lying on as a permanent sun-trap

You do not see it often, but I include it regularly: a broad seat as the border along a terrace, on which you can put pots, get rid of a tray of drinks or even sit on. You can also, and this is the point, lie on it in the sun. With a few cushions underneath you a broad, low wall is an excellent place for lying full-length and sunbathing or reading in the sun, or on a balmy afternoon, particularly after lunch and a few glasses of wine. The body is fully stretched out, which is good for

A group of tables and chairs on the grass is a wonderful place to sit in summer. In the spring and autumn it is a nuisance because the grass is often wet, and drier terraces are favoured. If you have to mow you will want separate pieces of furniture which you can move about.

the back muscles; you can relax totally and can face the world again after ten minutes.

If you like tranquil, austere lines it is best to put something flat on a wall like this. Buy a long piece of foam rubber the same length as the wall seat-cum-bed and cover it with a sheet which is removable and washable. If you want to do it absolutely perfectly you can put a piece of sailcloth or plastic underneath so that no colour comes off the sometimes rather damp wall. But this is not necessary because if a sheet gets dirty, if it has a zip or ties, it can soon be put in the washing machine. Material with blue squares, or green, white or ecru, or with narrow stripes are ideal.

Material for wall seats-cum-beds

Expensive, but particularly attractive, are walls made of brick. If you are building a new house the cost is trifling compared with the cost of the house. Piles can be driven into the ground at the same time on peaty soil or a concrete foundation can be laid on sandy ground. If you have an existing house and still want to put up walls of brick, the best solution is to dig the trench a bit wider than the wall, to a depth of 70cm (28in). At the bottom I lay an iron mesh and pour concrete over it. This layer hardens after a few days and the brick wall can be built on top of it. Often the wall is begun with sand-lime bricks and then continued with brick to about 15cm (6in) below the future lowest level of the earth, to allow for the ground to subside,

There are reclining chairs for sunbathing made of pulp cane, cane, wood and synthetic materials. Lay mattresses on top of them for hours of comfort.

which could result in the much lighter coloured sand-lime bricks becoming visible.

A blue bench creates a lively note in the Dekmans garden.

If you make a wide wall for lying on 60cm (24in) or so wide the foundation must also be slightly higher, for example 80cm (32in) for a concrete foundation. Build two walls of sand-lime bricks on this and when you have almost reached the top, pour sand between these two walls. Or you can leave a cavity as air space. The advantage can be that if there is a sharp frost you have no trouble with expanding sand, so no cracks can occur in the wall either. The moisture in sand or earth expands when it freezes and the forces which are summoned up are inconceivable, and many a wall, pond, and even house has suffered cracks and splits.

You can finish off the top of a wall in two ways. A flat top can be made, which means that the sides are flat all the way up. Or you can make a slightly overlapping clinker edge. The latter is nicer with old-fashioned houses and the former with modern architecture where the romantic would look wrong.

Always try to bring the wall seats into harmony with the house as regards colour, or, alternatively, let them form a contrast to it. With new buildings, choose the same materials for the walls of house and garden and for the steps of a flight of steps in the garden. If you have an old house and want to build a new wall it is definitely worth taking the trouble to look for matching stone. If you are not successful then you could look for a much darker stone for the stairs, steps and walls.

Do not forget that new stones get darker, so a brick, which according to your supplier matches your house but which looks too light to you, will begin to take on a nice bit of colour after a few rain showers, and after a few years will have become practically the same dark colour as the stones of your house. Take photos of your house and take them with you, because very often there is not so much as a loose brick left from the old house.

Wooden boards on stone walls

Stone absorbs moisture and that is why you must use special hard-baked outdoor brick for the garden. The softer stones for indoor work fall apart if they freeze: they crack when the moisture in the stone expands. This sort of wall can stay damp for a long time because moisture gets into the stone, so wooden boards are sometimes laid on this sort of wall. Wood dries out more quickly than stone, so the wall is ready for you to lie or sit on again sooner. If you like things to be "clean" you should varnish the wood or dip it in oil, then it will stay clean. If you leave wood to age it can also become rather greenish. But this is a question of what goes with your house.

If the window frames and doors are of oiled wood then dip your seats and reclining chairs in oil. If everything about the house is old

Here smooth-planed boards are used for a wooden platform. If the spot is sunny everything is fine. In very wet spots or those with a lot of shadow boards with chamfered edges should be used.

then choose the same for the outside bench. If it is all painted white, blue or green, then make sure you repeat this for the reclining bench. Then you will obtain the harmony you desire. The plants can then compensate for any severity.

A sunbathing wall by the water

Imagine: behind the house there is a small terrace and, a bit below, the large sitting terrace. Behind this is a large pond with abundantly growing plants. A wall for lying on has been built across half the width of the pond: you can lie on this and gaze dreamily into the water . . .

Wooden platforms

My method of sunbathing is to lay a mattress on a wooden platform, with a cushion under my head, so I do not need deckchairs or reclining chairs. I keep the mattresses in a restored hen-house. The black-stained platform makes a wonderfully protected spot, surrounded by the walls of the barn on my Zeeland farm, which are also black-stained or tarred, and it is ideal for sunbathing out of the wind. With the help of a gardener I am making a little pond on the south side of the platform terrace. There are already bamboo poles there. A bamboo pipe has been laid in the middle so that one side is hidden in the bamboo and the other end hangs above the new pond. A thin stream of water is going to come out of the pipe into the pond and create a constant soft tinkling noise. The water is pumped back to the bamboo pipe by a small pump, so it keeps circulating. Of course, electricity is necessary to enable pumping to take place.

Platforms as a theme in a platform garden in Utrecht

When you have been a landscape gardener for long enough you will have designed gardens several times for the same family. Usually family and landscape gardener begin with a small house and a small garden and small children. The next commission comes when the family moves to a bigger house. Fortunately the garden is usually bigger too. In the first stage I designed for my clients a platform which ran from the dining room right through the garden to the barn, with an asymmetrical division of the space. The platform widened out into terraces and narrowed down to paths. Large decorative leafy plants, such as tall ornamental reeds, *Miscanthus*, bamboo *(Arundinaria japonica)*, *Hosta*, and *Ligularia* inhabited the plant borders, which were mostly not very big.

When it was time for the owners to move, I designed another garden; again with platforms, not in a continuous form this time, but in squares which were all on different levels. A long wooden platform was placed near the high-level dining room on the already existing concrete floor. The stairs of concrete and small paving stones were covered in wood and thus became much more "relaxed".

The rest of the garden was divided into two. One part became a platform with the existing pond. The platform formed the link element with the second part of the garden: a more or less round lawn.

Facing page: Deckchairs are made of hardwood. They are designed to fold up, because they could not be left on deck in heavy storms and had to be put away. Place thick cushions on them, which are made to size, and you can lounge in them for hours.

For a house with modern shapes, where "classical" deckchairs look out of place, it is possible to choose reclining chairs with austere shapes, like these Italian chairs, which are not only beautiful, but also practical.

Round lines are either enclosed in themselves if you can see the whole of them at once, or they are infinite if you cannot see the end of them.

So if you lay a circle of grass so that you cannot see the whole edge, it seems as if the line is infinite. If you sit in the circle of grass and you can see all the sides, a feeling of security is created.

The round lawn was chosen for the new garden as a contrast to the straight shape of the platforms, with *Hosta*, bamboo, holly, and autumn anemones round it. In among these are tall trees, such as ash, cherry, and ornamental apple. Some clumps of ornamental grass and white roses were put in beside the platforms, and, at the express and correct request of the owners, large butterbur, *Gunnera*, and *Darmera peltata* combined with *Lamiastrum galeobdolon*, the colourful deadnettle, which allows silvery swathes of leaves to grow between the large green leaves of the other plants.

A luxurious world of decorative greenery has been created by these large round leaves and by lots of tall bamboo, *Phyllostachys aurea*, combined with the rigid shapes of wood and grass.

The platforms are used for lying and sitting on. You sit at a round wooden table with a gigantic parasol in the middle, which makes eating outside possible even in the rain. Comfortable cane seats stand around it. If you feel like it you can lie on the platforms, which, since they are at different heights, do not appear massive, but are broken up into several cosy terraces, which quickly become dry and warm. Because of the gaps between the wood the whole remains transparent and airy. Pergolas, overgrown with grapes, form the transition from house to garden. Later the front and side gardens were tackled too, so now harmony has been created in the shape of terraces and lines.

The front garden   I laid a large terrace, which was originally also supposed to be made of wood, in front of the part of the house which juts out. However, it was found to be too dangerous for elderly visitors, so it was made of elongated small-headed bricks. These were given the same reddish colour as the house.

Between the terrace and the wall I put a narrow strip with very tall bamboos, *Phyllostachys* again. Then the path fans out on the left to a front door and on the right to an enclosed bicycle shed. Cobblestones are used here as paving.

There are some steps and hedges, all in a straight line, with just white flowering roses planted in between, combined with large butterbur, ornamental grass and *Lamium*, the colourful deadnettle. It is a simple planting experiment, but very effective and striking. I chose the *Catalpa bignonioides* 'Nana' as a tree, which produces large, oval, light green leaves. These trees stand in a long double row in front of the façade in the front garden and bring harmony to the various shapes of the garden.

This wall seat was created for a modern garden. The pond is on the left at a higher level and I created the hollowed-out sitting area so that you can see over the top of the furniture. The wall seat is also a boundary wall. Boards have been fixed on to it so that you can sit in the dry.

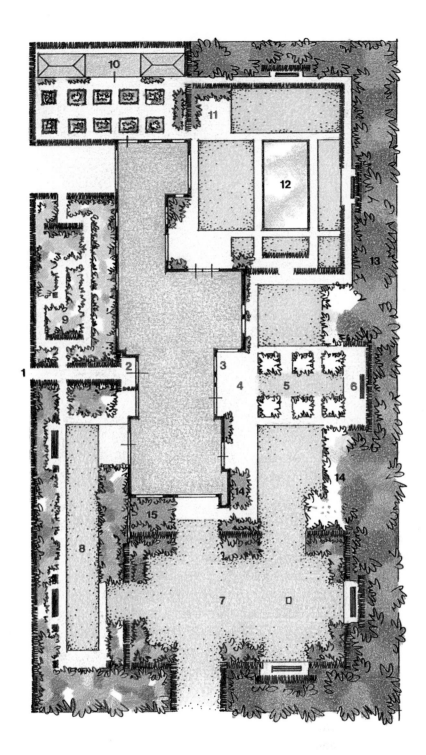

1 public path

2 house entrance

3 spacious hall with view on to 4

4 the white garden with a spacious terrace for fine pots and cane furniture from Thailand

5 in the white garden lots of standard roses and perennials and for each section a block of yew for dramatic winter effect

6 tables and chairs with Lutyens bench

7 amber-coloured rose garden surrounded by yew hedges with view from below of a public park; hedge and small pond are added for protection

8 blue garden with iron arches from left to right across the grass path

9 pink garden with arches overgrown with fruit trees

10 new glasshouse in dark green aluminium (design A. J. van der Horst), in front a colourful garden of flowers for cutting

Pergolas and garden buildings

Sometimes there should be an architectural transition from house to garden, in which case a pergola is often built. If this is attached to the house, it forms a very clear link with the garden.

A wooded garden with a pergola

However, this does not always have to be the case. Sometimes pergolas can be placed elsewhere in the garden, away from the house, for the express purpose of creating a new architectural emphasis to break up all the greenery. This fascinates me. Recently I designed a spacious wooded garden and put a pergola in the wood.

If you have a large area of land it can be important to build a summer-house or pergola a long way from the house, but still visible, which harmonizes with the size, colour, material and character of the house. The house is, as it were, repeated in the garden and a new area of suspense is created. I used this design in a mature wooded garden with tall single pines and broad, low-branched beeches and a long row of tall rhododendrons to enclose the longest side of the garden.

Deep inside the garden I put a long straight pond the same width as the rear elevation of the modern, white-painted house. The disadvantage of water which is far away is that you can hardly see anything of it.

For this reason I had a little wall built with little freestone water chutes, out of which the water falls into the pond. You can see this from the house and from the well-proportioned kitchen terrace. A large terrace with a substantial pergola was laid around the tall single pines to bring an end to the long architectural shape of the water.

The whole thing introduces sharp horizontal lines into an area

Beehives must be kept dry, which can be achieved by putting them under a lean-to. Put in plants which look pretty and have flowers to provide food for the bees, and both man and bee will be content.

which was of decidedly vertical character, mainly owing to the rising shapes of the pines.

Since the house has white walls and black-stained wooden doors and window frames, in my opinion the pergola ought to be black too. The clients feel more inclined so far, however, to let the wood age naturally. White wisteria, *Wisteria sinensis* 'Alba', which is already starting to shoot, grows up against it. The collection of beeches provides another broad and graceful element and gives balance; these are quite young specimens of twenty years old or so, which have not yet been cut back and therefore hang with their elegant branches over the grass and the newly flowering plants. A tranquil linking element is created by the large flat area of the perfect smooth-mown lawn, which remains green in summer and winter. It is the same with the *Taxus baccata* hedge, which was placed like a large hook round the pond and the terrace.

This is of course a large area. But it can also be done on a small scale. I once designed a romantic rose garden. I was given a square piece of ground that was enclosed on four sides by yew hedges. In the middle of this green space I designed an octagonal summerhouse; it was composed of eight splendid octagonal posts, with a board at the bottom, on the inside and the outside. I allowed all sorts of old-fashioned and modern climbing roses to grow up against it, combined with *Clematis* varieties, which bloom at different times

Rose arches have been erected in this garden in the old centre of 's-Hertogenbosch to form a leafy corridor, with box and orange trees in pots on the terrace.

of the year. Its success was due in part to the four small benches which I had fixed to the posts in the summer-house. These were hanging benches without backs to provide somewhere to sit and look at the splendid flowers. I designed four flower-beds around the octagonal summer-house, which were planted with long-flowering plants, such as *Lavatera olbia* 'Rosea' and *Polygonum amplexicaule*. There were more roses and violets in beds all around. I used clinkers as paving for the whole garden. The octagonal shape means that it does not directly relate to anything else. Certainly not with the house, though it does with the garden. This is therefore a good model if you just want a summer-house somewhere without its having any direct connection with the shape of the house.

Sometimes a shady sitting area like this appears to develops all on its own. If you are sensible you will begin with a water-tight roof, so that you can sit in the dry; then the plants can grow and be trimmed by shears.

Shapes for pergolas There was a time when architects did everything possible to integrate house and garden architecturally with one another. This happened especially in the "back to nature" movement at the end of the last century. In England this was given the splendid name of "Arts and Crafts". Arts and crafts were supposed to be inspired, according to the new rules of the time, by nature itself and by the architecture of farms. The architecture of this period often seems to have grown from the environment. Rural, country, and home-made products took precedence over anything produced in a factory and you could hear the sound of protest against decline, drabness, and exploitation by industrial developers. In architectural schools they were keen to interpret the rural, for example, by building a lot of garden walls, by connecting the house with the garden by means of pergolas, by erecting summer-houses and including a lot of brick steps and long ponds. At De Hooge Vuursche castle, at the nature reserve of the same name between Hilversum and Baarn, the Netherlands, you can see this style in a garden lay-out of great allure. Since the houses were mostly of brick or natural stone and everything was built to last forever, the same materials, brick and freestone, were used for the columns of the pergola. The shape of these columns was often square, which fitted in with the flat façades of the houses. Wooden beams were placed on these columns, over which roses, blue wisteria and *Aristolochia* were trained.

Many architects and landscape gardeners were fascinated by this and thought it was a good way to integrate house and garden. Dick Tersteeg is probably the most proficient at this idea and his pergolas of brick with wooden beams are generally admired. Leonard Springer also knew how to bring about this integration. Leonard van der Putten is a less well-known landscape gardener, but he was certainly skilful, especially in matching the supports of the pergolas.

In this garden in St-Truiden in Belgium I designed a pergola with a roof of reinforced glass to make a dry walkway from the studio to the house.

Stone pergola supports   In Oegstgeest, near Leiden, you can enjoy a wonderful garden at the De Beukenhof restaurant. There is a large ancient beech standing

next to the white farm-like restaurant. In a masterly gesture a hook-shaped pergola has been built, which begins at a corner of the building, runs into the garden and then goes round a corner and ends next to the beech.

A large part of the garden is enclosed by pergola, house, and garden. The line of the pergola is followed by a pond which is also hook-shaped. Next to the house-cum-restaurant stands the large terrace, which is closed off by a wall at the back. The part of the pergola and the pond which runs towards the beech is lined with a special border of perennials. There are purple roses and bright blue flowers. *Bergenia*, *Anchusa* and *Hesperes* are responsible for the spectacle seen here.

The pergola is made so that you can walk underneath it. The broad square columns are painted white, the beams, which are ageing naturally, just have blue wisteria, *Wisteria sinensis*, growing over them.

Cut wisteria sharply back and leave the small shoots with the flower buds, so that first the flowers and later the leaves amply cover sturdy pergolas.

A pergola garden by Leonard van der Putten

This landscape gardener, who has become famous as a restaurateur, designed a private garden in Geleen for the director of the Dutch state mines. The garden was not actually very large, but contained many surprises.

There was, for example, a substantial terrace and, situated a bit lower, a rectangular lawn with a magnificent border along it with pink *Ceanothus*, *Campanula lactiflora* 'Loddon Anna', *Salvia*

nemorosa 'East Friesland', with cream and pink phlox and blue violets in the foreground. All sorts of delicate colours followed on from one another. The border, which could be seen from the house, ended in a long pergola which was built at the back of the garden across the whole width. This pergola also had stone pillars, not of natural stone, but of brick with wooden boards on top. Blue wisteria and *Rosa* 'New Dawn' grew here. What I noticed here and in De Beukenhof was the fact that the sturdy brick-built pillars in no way looked heavy. This happens much more with heavy wooden posts. It could also be that the heavy wooden beams which had been put lengthways and crossways over the top of them gave enough counterbalance, so that the supports did not look out of place. Here, too, blue wisteria was a good choice of fanciful climber to lend elegance to the sturdy structure and to heighten the sense of the dramatic with its long clusters.

Besides this pergola, under which grass had been sown, which gave a good impression of space, there was still more to discover. For example, there was a long pond on the other side of the lawn and there was a long grass track with yew arches. *Taxus baccata* 'Fastigiata Aurea' is a golden yellow yew which grows in the shape of pillars. If you cut them well they stay in pillar shapes and you can even just about make an arch out of them by training both tops across an iron arch. Arches like this were spectacularly trained a

I designed this covered sitting area, which was first painted white and later ochre, at a Utrecht farm. It is a special delight with its tasteful decorative plants, pots, and seats.

41

number of times across the long grass track. So you could see here something of the versatility of Leonard van der Putten, whose work was well-known; you can still see his own garden at the Oegstgeest restaurant, De Beukenhof. It is perfectly kept by a team of permanent gardeners, one of whom was trained by Van der Putten himself. This gardener has been looking after the garden for more than twenty-five years.

Roofs and summer-houses

I am myself a great lover of places where you can leave all the garden things outside when it rains. The idea of finding everything dry after an unexpected shower of rain, the table with its cloth, the bench with its cushions, the chairs and the flowers not drenched with rain, is a blessing. Everyone who has visited countries which are longing for rain says that countries which have a lot of rain are lucky.

But the disadvantage of so much rain, in the summer too, is that you never know when a shower like that is coming. You can even be doing something at the bottom of the garden and be surprised by a sudden downpour, which leaves all the cushions soaked through.

A covered pergola

I have already talked about the different ways of constructing pergolas: with stone, pillars, or wooden posts. However, if you are making a covered pergola it needs to be rather more strongly constructed, because the roof consists of a structure of panels, roof tiles, thick reinforced glass, or corrugated sheet metal, as well as beams.

Corrugated sheet metal is a good covering, but it looks ugly, unless you disguise the underside of the corrugated metal to some extent with a solid trelliswork, ecru-coloured tarpaulin, rush mats, or thin wooden boards, which fit into each other with tongue and groove. If you grow some sort of evergreen on top of the corrugated metal, for example *Lonicera peryclimenum* 'Belgica', which has yellowy white flowers, the ugliness of the material is easily disguised.

Though if you need to go to so much trouble, you may wonder if there are no other possibilities.

Plywood roof panels

I work a lot with pergolas which have a roof of plywood panels. You can cover the outside with a layer of blackish grey asphalt paper and the underside of the plywood, which you can see, can be stained or painted grey-blue, grey-green, yellow ochre, or ox-blood red with outdoor stain.

If you like things simple you can keep the natural wood colour and try to train an ivy along it. This is most successful, because the evergreen *Hedera*, once it has been trained to roof height, likes shadow and will therefore seek out the wood. The plywood is fastened to the pergolas, so that you can still see the beams on the inside.

My favourite: a glass roof

For places where ordinary glass may be too easily knocked and broken another sort of glass has been developed: glass with iron threads in it. You can imagine the production process: glass is poured on to a meshwork of thin iron, the whole thing hardens and the iron is sealed in and airtight. I have heard it said more than once by experts that the outsides of this threadwork, where the glass plate stops, would rust and cause problems, but I have never noticed this so far. Be that as it may, I have put this glass successfully on many pergolas. Snow has not caused it to break, nor leaves which have accumulated from above, nor heavy bundles of climbing plants lying on top of it. All the same, I try to be careful with climbing plants on the roof. Glass is after all transparent. Climbing plants lose their leaves, which fall on the glass and are almost impossible to remove. A high pressure hose is the only thing for this.

A summer-house roof

If what you admire most of all is roses in bloom you will enjoy sitting beneath them and watching how their clusters of flowers shimmer in profusion in the sun. The solution is to build a summer-house with an open roof.

I built a pergola with an open roof for the "Floriade" in Zoetermeer; roses can swirl over the top of it in great profusion because the structure is extremely strong. This is why most summer-houses with roses are made of hardwood: it does not rot and can still bear the weight of the load when it gets heavy and wet, even after years of damp earth around the supports. You see splendid summer-houses

The imposing proportions of the leafy avenue of wood and beech in the garden of Het Loo palace.

in England, much more romantic than the ones in the Netherlands. The entrances to these are often arches of trelliswork and the trelliswork or horizontal supports of the roof are so close together that the pink creepers remain hanging in between them. At the Scottish castle of Tyninghame I once saw one in mauve-blue with red roses and mauve-blue *Clematis* 'Lasurstern'. You could copy this example, since, apart from anything else, the materials remain within financial limits because of its open style.

Garden sheds must fit into the design as a whole; then they become an ornament instead of something which has to be designed to be kept out of sight. Here is my solution at Huis Ten Bosch near Maarssen.

The designs of Jan van der Groen

One of the most interesting books about historical gardens is the book which Prince Frederick Henry's gardener wrote on three subjects: gardens, keeping bees, and good housekeeping. The first subject particularly interests me. This well-read man, whom it is difficult to imagine as one of the hundreds of gardeners in the service of the prince, was well informed about the latest developments in France, where an enthusiastic and very successful garden design family, the Mollet dynasty, was at work.

He adopted many of their designs for flat areas of garden with small hedges, flowers, and stone chippings. I am convinced that he also drew designs himself. What fascinates me is the series of trelliswork structures and summer-houses which he drew for the book: simple structures or, especially with the trelliswork, exuberant baroque constructions with arches, points and complicated patterns. His

series of summer-houses excels by simplicity, which is easy to explain. In his day, the sixteenth and seventeenth centuries, the medieval idea of the green summer-house was still in vogue. A simple structure was built and beech, hornbeam, or hawthorn was trained across the top of it. The branches of these hedge plants were trained across the top of the wooden structure following the shape of the square, octagonal, or elongated summer-house and the result was a summer-house covered in foliage. You still find these in old drawings, engravings, and paintings.

Two of these green summer-houses stood in the back garden at Huis ten Bosch in the Hague. They had even been extended to two floors high. You can still copy this idea now, as it is only a question of putting in tall plants, having patience, and of course skilful handling of the pruning knife. If you start with so-called pivots, long continuous stems with short side branches down to the bottom, and plant them quite closely together you can have a summer-house like this of 3 to 4m (10–13ft) in height thickly covered in three years. It would be good to try a summer-house like this if you like sitting in the shade. If you choose the beech, *Fagus sylvatica*, you are assured of a summer-house with green leaves in the summer and brown in the winter, because beech does not lose its leaves. They fall in the spring when the young leaves first appear.

A straight pergola has grapes growing over it to create a shady roof at the end of the long pond. The wooden table is decorated with vases. The view through to the farmland is exquisite.

An open wooden summer-house at Menkema castle

If you need inspiration before you begin on your own summer-house, a good place to visit is the garden of Menkema castle in Uithuizen in the province of Groningen. Here an open summer-house has been built of hardwood with horizontal slats as a roof. Roses grow through these in luxurious profusion. The garden is worth seeing as an example of a Renaissance garden, which has been completely newly laid out.

You can experience the ideas of Jan van der Groen in this luxurious formal, though certainly not boring, garden.

Closed summer-houses/garden sheds

If you are thinking of having a summer-house you usually have a set idea in mind. For me this is an octagonal basic shape for the walls, with a pointed roof on top. I have put many of these in gardens already. They mostly have glass on three or five sides and are closed at the back, because I usually place summer-houses like this at the end of the garden, from where you can have a splendid view across the garden. The advantage of a division like this is that you have a plain back wall for a bench or chairs.

This has been splendidly thought out in a formal garden in Wijchen, where a little antique Spanish table of greyish painted wood has been placed. Cane chairs were added and a small freestone sink with a fine tap, so that you can make tea. This spot lies in the centre of the sight-line which runs through the formal garden.

When I designed this garden, which was all in shades of pink, blue, and grey, I already knew that this would be the pinnacle of the whole garden. I put a wall behind the summer-house with a semi-circular pond in the wall to the left and the right of the summer-house, raised like a basin. A fountain has been mounted above the basin so that the water can circulate and a decorative stream of water comes out of the fountain and falls into the basin. Sitting in the summer-house you can thus hear the soft splatter of the water.

There are fragrant roses, lavender, and seedlings, which together create an atmosphere of fanciful formality. It was decided to make the paintwork white, but it would probably have been better if it had been more greyish in colour. This has been resolved with climbing plants which soften the white.

New with a centuries-old aura

There was an old farmhouse which was overlooked from the road. To stop people looking in, a thick wall was combined with the construction of a summer-house. A wooden framework of supports was made of salvaged wood, in other words old used boards, and a pointed roof with sloping beams, on which grey roof tiles were placed. Feathered boards were used for the back: you begin with the bottom horizontal board and then let the following slightly higher board overlap the last one slightly. Then water runs from board to board without being able to get inside. The sides were made of trelliswork. Everything was painted black outside and greyish blue inside. All kinds of wreaths made of box, olive branches and fir cones were put up on the inner wall, which made the walls look old. Dried strings of hops were hung from the roof and rush chairs were placed at a round table. This extremely comfortable summer-house, which looks centuries old, is used more for sitting in in the summer than the splendid farmland, because you can sit protected, out of the wind and rain, and still be outside. Obviously not everyone can manage to get salvaged wood. If you are not good at making things, it would be best to ask a carpenter to make the structure, as roof tiles are heavy and the human head is vulnerable.

Conservatories to sit in

I love conservatories and glasshouses you can sit in. There are various ways of keeping out the summer heat. For instance, you can put a wooden roller consisting of horizontal slats attached to each other on the roof, at least in the summer when the sun is at its fiercest. In the winter you can roll up a screen like this and allow the sun to warm the glasshouse or conservatory. If you do not want a screen you can train vines over the outside of the roof. This creates a green roof in the summer with bunches of grapes ripening in the heat.

If all this is not enough for you or you reject both solutions, you could consider curtains or "Venetian blinds", which are fixed to the inside of the roof.

You see good use of these in Greece, France, Italy, and Spain,

The long backs and comfortable seats make these classic garden chairs very popular. Here they match the white of the pergola and the light floor tiles.

because in these countries it is the most natural thing in the world to put in some sort of protection against the sun.

In a glasshouse you can pull a cloth along tensioned wires using rings attached or built into it. You can pull up a screen like this with cords on the rings or just let it drop. "Venetian blinds" work like this: here too you use rings on the sides of the screen. The difference is in the horizontal slats which are sewn into the cloth. These make the cloth stiffer so the whole thing looks much nicer, whether it is fully up or half pulled up.

The most neutral thing to use is white or ecru-coloured cloth, which does not have to be thick to keep out the heat. And it can always be removed if not required.

The glasshouse should occasionally be cooled and ventilated, hence the little windows in the roof which you open to let the air circulate. There are also windows with sections of glass which you can open. These are a kind of glass laminate. This is also a good method of ventilation. A "breeze" caused by a large fan turning lends a tropical atmosphere. It is clear if you study the circumstances in which conservatory and greenhouse plants grow in the wild that it is a good thing not only to protect oneself against the sun's rays, but also, and in particular, the plants: they often grow in rain forests or in the shadow of tall palms, so the leaves are only slightly exposed to the direct rays of the sun. This is the reason why, for as long as there have been glasshouses, people have looked for ways of keeping out this heat and the burning effect of the sun. This is why nearly all professional glasshouses are whitewashed: to keep out direct sunlight, but still to let light through.

You can do this on the inside of your roof too, if nothing else works. You sluice it off in the autumn with a ceiling mop or a brush on a stick.

Laminated panels on the roof An extension was built onto the north side of a house in a large garden in Sassenheim. This semicircular extension apparently got too hot when the sun was above the house and shone in through the glass. So the owners tried everything they could to find a way to refract the rays of the sun.

Finally the solution turned out to be to install vertical partitions which were at the right height to intercept the sun. An advantage of this system is that you can look out from inside and see the light, which would not be possible with curtains.

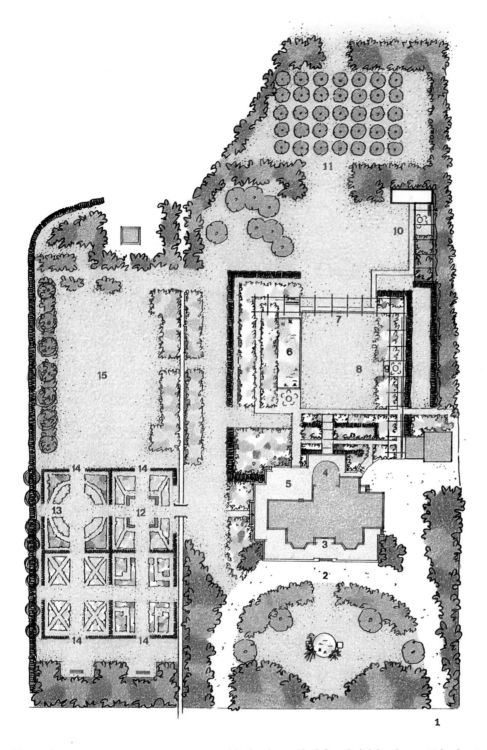

A garden in Sassenheim

1 public road

2 front garden with gravel path running around it and round pond in the grass with two lead common cranes

3 white entrance laid with bricks

4 new conservatory with view of the back garden

5 spacious high-level terrace

6 low-lying pond garden with yellow and white border on the left and pink border on the right

7 pergola with blue wisteria and roses

8 a large sundial on the lawn

9 small terrace with sandstone bench and table

10 shady terrace with barn, screening and pergola

11 orchard

12 lead water-trough on a pedestal with two lead doves in the amber-coloured and yellow rose garden

13 a green wooden bench with wrought iron frame in a garden of pink and blue perennials

14 dark green iron arches

15 playing field

Summer-houses

At the beginning of this century it was

fashionable to make pergolas and summer-houses from the same materials as those used in the construction of the house. There are many examples in England and France.

The stone summer-house of Tintinhull House

You can build fine, roofed garden seating areas with stone, as I found out when I visited the garden of Tintinhull House in England. One section of the garden was crowned by a simple, but attractive summer-house with two stone pillars which supported the roof on the side which looked onto the garden. It brought a dignified conclusion to the "drama" evoked here. Following on from the summer-house, which was closed off at the back and the sides, a long straight pond had been built, which lay like a mirror amongst the grass. To the left and right of the grass were broad borders of perennials with hedges behind as a wall. The borders were designed by Penelope Hobhouse, who wielded the sceptre here on behalf of the National Trust. She chose warm colours, purple, violet and orange, to demonstrate how these can be used. Four rather pale sand-coloured terracotta pots were almost the same colour as the stone pillars of the summer-house. The round pillars showed up well, owing to the severity of the rest of the shapes in this area.

The sandstone colour is right for England, where many tiles and ornaments and even houses are made of this soft sort of stone. The pillars are made of sandstone mixed with cement by specialists and are available in many sizes. These are good materials which go green relatively quickly, whether or not helped by a considerable quantity of buttermilk which is painted onto the pillars. On top of the pillars, put wood which can be left to age, hardwood in other words, and

This neo-classical sandstone summer-house, which stands in Rosemary Verey's garden at Barnsley House, in Gloucestershire, fits in well with a large green garden or with a historic house and garden, but not in an area of modern buildings.

then decide whether you want a flat or a pointed roof. With a flat roof you must make sure the water can escape at the back, so the roof must slope slightly to that side. A small copper, zinc, or lead gutter is, of course, an excellent idea. If you want a pointed roof you must construct the roof with rafters which run at an angle and another beam where they meet. Roof tiles, preferably old ones which have already weathered a bit, are put on this sort of roof. Grey tiles are rather sombre, terracotta-coloured ones are warm, while bright red roof tiles give a rustic feel. If you want something special and at the same time neutral you can choose wooden roof tiles or slates.

Wooden roof tiles, slates, and zinc

In America, wooden roof tiles are used on houses, barns, and anything which needs roofing, because wood is cheap there. Often there is no clay, which is why hardwood roof tiles are often used and are made to overlap each other. The advantage is that they weather to a striking pale greyish green colour. I first saw them used in the Netherlands around Maastricht. They looked splendid. The slates were laid in such a way that the bottom of one slate always overlapped the top of the slate below; this way you have no problems with water coming in. In Japan I saw wooden roof tiles like these used for garden gates which were supposed to look old. Moss soon grew on them, and sometimes ferns too. This could also be achieved by making a bamboo gutter, in which earth containing young fern plants is placed; in

The garden house of Wylre Castle, Limburg, after the owner had carried out his ideas of integration with the garden.

other words not a gutter to take the water away, but a plant border. All churches, or at least many of them, are roofed with slates. The thin slates are hung and overlap each other. They are grey and elegant. In Heerlen, in the garden of a house of great beauty, which is hundreds of years old, a view has been created through the garden, at the end of which stands a little summer-house roofed with slates. It is octagonal, has a pointed slate roof and is further embellished with white-painted trelliswork. This little summer-house is a dream and just one example of the numerous possible variations, for instance dark green trelliswork and little wooden tiles on the roof or a zinc roof which quickly fades and goes well with a house with a grey tiled roof.

An open summer-house with a thatched roof stands in a garden in Kloetinge in Zeeland; in front of it the meadow of flowers is mown only once a year.

An iron summer-house

I once designed the garden of an old farmhouse with a number of stone courtyards as permanent seating and display areas, since the garden was not only for private use, but also for exhibiting statues. For both purposes I designed two courtyards. One was directly behind the house, really as a courtyard for a large table with chairs, large statues, and possibly pots with annuals and globes of box.

This became an open, sunny courtyard, from which you can see a large pond with a lot of hortensias. In the left-hand corner of this large courtyard was a sitting area for private use. Above this I built an iron summer-house with a split roof, for the following reason. A normal pointed roof, which has the same sloping surface on four sides, runs in one line towards the point. A split roof breaks up this straight line, so that a sloping part, a straight part and then another straight part is created going up to the pitch of the roof. I had this made in iron bands which were galvanized against rust and painted dark green. The whole thing was carefully planned so that, working with straight lines, you obtain a finer structure in the roof parts and the straight walls. Sometimes the strips are horizontal and vertical and straight open squares are created, and sometimes sloping lines were fixed on top of each other. I grew white wisteria over the iron bands, the clusters of which hung from the roof downwards. The combined effect is restful; it is a genuine green summer-house which in time gives more and more shade as the branches of the climbers begin to spread in all directions.

This is a large summer-house enclosing a square terrace of 5 x 5m (16 x 16ft). Around it I planted white-flowering wisteria as well as the rose 'Virgo', which blooms with large white flowers, and 'Schneewittchen', a bright white cluster rose. Other white-flowering perennials were added. Box hedges formed an evergreen border around the flowers. This large summer-house was later made in a slightly smaller size of 4 x 4m (13 x 13ft). Both sizes can be roofed with glass. Make sure the ironwork is galvanized, so that it cannot rust. Preferably paint ironwork in dark colours, then it makes a gossamer-fine dark play of lines against the sky, which is taken up by the climbing plants.

You will find sun and shade here at all times of the day. The roof tiles are square and flat, the woodwork is white.

A bench and pot are placed next to one of the outhouses in this garden. The walls are white plastered and the tiles are red and flat (Giardini, Belgium).

A green summer-house

At Genk in Belgium there is a magnificent garden. It consists of many sections, but can be roughly divided into a front and a back part. The front part is directly behind the rear elevation of the very wide house with a terrace and lawns. Leading from the door to the garden is a path of freestone tiles, grey with little yellow stones round them. At the end of this path there is a striking green summer-house, which already existed in the garden, made of cornelian cherry, *Cornus mas*, which has been pruned into a wall with three arches. The arches lead the wanderer to a cool summer-house which is green in the summer; in the winter it is bare and brown, and in the spring light yellow.

At this season the summer-house is a powerful eye-catcher, which cannot be matched. When you plant these shrubs you realize that this is something which you can grow quite quickly. They grow quite fast, after a rather hesitant start, and tall: a good 4m (13ft) if you do not watch out. To be on the safe side make an iron or wooden frame, as our ancestors did when they wanted to create a green summer-house. Other shrubs suitable for this are *Forsythia*, which grows just as quickly and will bloom slightly later with a rather more vivid yellow, and pink-flowering *Kolkwitzia*. All *Spiraeas* can be pruned into hedges and therefore also into summer-houses, as can apples, pears, morello cherries, and figs. There are therefore plenty of opportunities for something spectacular like this in your garden.

In the historic garden of Wylre Castle, Limburg, the owner had the little wooden summer-house restored. On one side you get the sun. This is a good example for anyone who wants something simple, but also romantic, in the way of a roofed terrace.

Water, a source of inspiration

One of the most delightful spots in my garden in Zeeland is where a piece of railway sleeper has been laid on top of a pile of paving stones to serve as a bench. I can sit there gazing at a long straight pond.

The pond is 17m (56ft) in length and 1.4m (4ft 6in) wide – in other words long and narrow, and therefore very impressive. At the end I placed an ornament, a man's head with a beard, which came from an old church. To the left and right of the pond there are going to be all sorts of things. This year I planted pumpkins and cucumbers beside it, and red cabbage at the corners of the pond. It is not going to stay like this; there are going to be scented flowering medicinal plants around it. You can see in old gardens how water can be used in a completely different way, not just as a long mirror.

The garden of Villa d'Este

Not far from Rome is one of the oldest and best-kept water gardens you could have as inspiration. The name is Villa d'Este, which comes from its most famous owner, Cardinal Ippolito d'Este. He lived in the fifteenth century, a time of great cultural blossoming in Italy, when cardinals and bishops led an almost wordly life of luxury in palaces with gardens and festivities.

Ippolito came from an illustrious family of princes and the descendants of emperors. When he had decided where he wanted to have his summer palace, a renowned engineer was asked to provide water for it. This engineer, who was named Ligorio, did this by energetically bringing a small river to the highest point of the garden, so that there was enough running water to create a water garden. A number of things could not be changed: the palace was situated high up and

A park with ancient trees provides the necessary shade in the garden of Aranjuez, the country residence of Spanish kings. In open places in avenues which intersect each other are attractive figures like this little boy pulling a thorn out of the sole of his foot, in a bronze fountain providing a cool oasis.

the garden was low down, so walls and steps had to be built to cater for the difference in height. This did not prove to be an insurmountable difficulty; the steep slope beneath the palace was transformed into a large terrace with steps. If you turned right at the bottom of these steps, you walked alongside a wall where water spurted from hundreds of little fountains into water troughs. The wall was embellished with eagles, a symbol of Ippolito's royal descent. When you have walked along this wall, which is completely moss-covered after hundreds of years of moisture, you stand eye to eye with a wall of the same height as that of the palace, from which all kinds of waterfalls and fountains fall to the ground. This is called a water organ, because there are, as with an organ, hard, strong notes (jets of water) and delicate notes (a fine spray of water).

It is fascinating to look at this and wonder how it is possible to achieve so many different effects with falling water. A large jet was caused by feeding the water through a thick pipe, and delicate trickles were created by numerous small holes. Ligorio certainly knew how to entrance visitors and his cardinal. This water device is still unparalleled in the world, especially as it comes as such a complete surprise after the visitor has just been admiring the hundreds of little fountains in the long wall.

There is more to see in this garden. I left you mentally turning right after you had descended the steep steps from the palace to the garden.

A pond does not have to be large. A small area for a marsh marigold, a water lily and a few special marsh plants is quite sufficient. You can buy small prefabricated ponds, water barrels, and lengths of plastic sheeting; the edges of these need to be well disguised.

If you go straight on, however, you can see long ponds to the left and the right, which reflect the light of the sun and the trees like mirrors. Formerly, in Ippolito's time, there were only small trees cut into round shapes, so the whole garden was bathed in sunlight. Now there are tall cypresses, which introduce a splendid vertical element into the horizontal image of the garden with its long flat ponds, paths, and walls. What I learned here was the magic of the long ponds which reflect the sun while remaining practically motionless. They form a contrast with falling water which makes a constant noise. The greatest ideas from this sort of garden should always be converted into our own much smaller scale of private garden today; the results will invariably be simple, but can often look very effective.

For instance, I converted the long ponds of the Villa d'Este into my 17m (56ft) long and 1.4m (4ft 6in) wide pond. I converted the wall with the hundreds of little fountains in the gardens of my clients by inserting little freestone chutes in walls. Here it was important not to copy indiscriminately, but to interpret to the heart's content to convert particular objects into new small-scale features.

Water in a miniature marsh garden   Anyone can have a miniature marsh garden, whether rich or poor. You need a watertight vessel, best of all half a wooden barrel, some water, and a nice selection of water or marsh plants. I have had a

This elegantly arched bridge could have come from a Chinese garden. The rocks next to it create this impression. The rest of the garden is luxuriant, with a rare mixture of light colours.

Campanula (blue) and lady's mantle (yellow) grow happily between slabs of freestone paving. If you want greater variation, sow thyme or violets, or stand a pot of lilies beside them. If you first dig a hole for the pot, the flowers in bloom will make a fine display on top of the paving.

wooden barrel like this, which I once bought at a garden centre, for more than fifteen years. I put a layer of polyester inside so that the barrel stayed watertight and, an incidental but important advantage, could not rot either. I put some earth in the bottom of the barrel and planted a yellow iris in it, which after all these years still flourishes luxuriantly. All sorts of things have been put in with it, such as marsh marigold (*Caltha palustris*) and water plantain (*Alisma plantago-aquatica*), which has been pushed out by the yellow iris after contributing to the pleasure of the marsh garden for years. For I must say: with a large pond you can enjoy the reflection of the water and large groups of plants, but the nice thing about a minia-ture swamp garden is that it is right beside the place where you sit. That is the idea: you group one or several of these barrels round a table and chairs, so that you are surrounded by the luxuriant shapes of the marsh plants.

If you prefer water lilies do not fill the vessel to 10 to 20cm (4 to 8in) below the level of the top, but put a layer of only about 15cm (6in) at the bottom. Depending on the height of the container you can plant a small water lily or a wild, white-flowering water lily. A depth of 40cm (16in) is sufficient for *Nymphaea pygmaea* 'Alba' to sur-vive; the wild water lily, *Nymphaea alba* needs to be deeper; a depth of 70cm (28in) is ideal for the large-leafed wild *Nymphaea*. *N. pygmaea* has smaller leaves. In a barrel the wild water lily will

The architect Gaudi could have designed this waterfall and I would love to have introduced the "softening" effect of plants.

soon fill the whole vessel, while *N. pygmaea* allows you to see water between the small round leaf shapes. If you like differently-coloured water lilies you can surround yourself with a whole collection in barrels right by the seating area. After all, they come in shades of yellow, orangey yellow, pink, and deep purple.

A little swamp garden in a stone trough

New or old, stone troughs are good articles to experiment with. They cannot be moved around easily, as these bluestone food containers are as heavy as lead. If you are able to get hold of one of these splendid feeding troughs make sure you know what you are doing. If you do not have a good wide pathway along the side of your house or a back entrance, then forget about having the trough on the back terrace. This is why they are usually seen at the front of the house. You can certainly put them here with the help of a lot of strong men or a machine.

A trough in a Maastricht town garden

In a garden which I designed with a large freestone terrace behind a house in Looiersplein in Maastricht, I stood a pair of large freestone feeding troughs on this terrace. I made one of them into a herb garden and the other into a marsh garden. With the herb garden there has to be an outlet for excess water, otherwise only marsh mint, meadowsweet, and purple loosestrife, *Lythrum salicaria*, will grow there. Apart from the wooden barrel and the freestone feeding

Wooden decking in the foreground, for sitting on, allows contact with the water. The plastic edge of the pond is hidden under the wood.

trough there are other materials which can be used for an attractive looking marsh garden, as you can use anything which is watertight. You sometimes see old zinc bathtubs used for this purpose, which look very nice. Plastic masonry tubs are also quite acceptable if they are luxuriantly planted, though they are not really very nice. If you collect wicker baskets you can put a watertight black plastic tub inside a basket and fill it with water and earth and then gather a whole series of water baskets around yourself.

Ponds with waterfalls

It may be technically difficult to make a pair of ponds flow into each other, but that is not to say it is impossible. I now have experience of a couple of possibilities for formal waterfalls. The first is a blue-stone slab which is mounted where the higher pond meets the lower pond. The water is allowed to flow over this. Naturally you must prevent the water in the higher pond from running away before it runs over the flat waterfall. This can be done by making the edges of the pond slightly higher at this point and those of the waterfall lower. A pump in the lower pond brings the water back up to the higher pond, which in principle creates continuous circulation.

I used a different system in a modern garden in Zeist, which was inspired by Japan. I had previously designed a garden for this modern house, but it proved necessary to adapt it when the opportunity arose to buy an additional piece of land on one side. I designed a large hook-shaped pond, which linked the old garden with the new land. One problem with this was that the old land was higher than the new land. So a waterfall had to be made in the hook-shaped pond. This was done with wood. A complicated structure is necessary, but it is possible.

The result is satisfying, owing to the harmony which it exudes. I combined large square wooden terraces and lots of gravel with the wooden waterfall. Along part of the boundary I put trelliswork with vertical slats. In front of this were clumps of bamboo, camellia and *Nandina domestica,* a fine-leafed shrub which has white flowers and red berries in the winter.

A splendid wooden waterfall in Groningen

It is always a new adventure to discover interesting gardens in totally unexpected places. This happened once in Groningen, in the village of Onstwedde. It lies in splendid spacious surroundings and the roads are lined with exceptionally large ancient oaks which have a wealth of leaves. An underground river apparently flowed here, which probably kept the roots of the oaks moist, so that they never suffered from lack of water. Two friends lived just outside this village. They had had to pull down their romantic little farmhouse and rebuild it and were surrounded by animals: goats, chickens, rabbits, and a rosy pink pig which was being fattened up in its pen. At the side and the back of their farm a hook-shaped pond had been dug out, which was on two levels. A waterfall linked the two parts of the

You can quickly achieve the effect of moss-covered garden statues that look as if they have been standing in the garden for decades by rubbing them with buttermilk.

pond. All round it were yellow-flowering plants, bushes, and tall *Miscanthus* and lots of *Hosta*. This is where I learned that it is possible to construct a waterfall with wooden boards.

A natural looking Japanese waterfall

In a country where the earth is covered by boulders you find a lot of people who know how to work with stone. This is often difficult in other countries, as people have no experience in piling up pieces of stone to look natural. But it can be successful.

First of all you must take a careful look at nature, seek out the mountains and look at waterfalls there. You often see a thin stream of water which has worn a narrow path between boulders. Then it falls, whether or not from a great height, usually in a thin jet. This is most spectacular if there is a protruding stone from which the water falls and there is a large distance from the waterfalls to where it trickles into a basin or a river flowing lower down. These are the things to remember: a striking effect is achieved in nature by a protruding stone which diverts the water, and a greater difference in height is more dramatic than a lesser one.

A waterfall in a river bed

In the mountains rivers often flow amongst the stones which they may or may not have loosened themselves by their grinding power. If you like mountains you will certainly like those clear mountain streams which sometimes have to bridge quite large differences in

In the evening light you can still see the water falling on the gravel. Underneath is a pond which catches the water, which is pumped back with a small pump.

height. This can give rise to lovely waterfalls, shaped by nature. Several large boulders stick out above the waterfall, between which the water trickles. This too is something to remember: water always seeks the lowest point, so if round stones are lying next to each other, the stream will flow in between the tallest parts of the stones. This can be imitated in a private garden, as long as you can get hold of large stones. If you take the trouble to go to a stone merchant you can sometimes find a wide choice of boulders from mountainous areas and from rivers. There are pretty, tranquil-coloured round stones in grey, bronze, or pinky shades and there are striking black stones. When I was laying out a large Japanese garden in Belgium I realized that you really have to go and look for yourself.

Pebbles and stones are used decoratively in this garden.

A waterfall in a Japanese garden in Belgium

It often seems strange as a Westerner to have to design and lay out a Japanese garden. And yet, how many Japanese do not play Western music or employ western architecture, clothing, or styles of furniture? This is why, after all those journeys to the "land of the rising sun", I have set about laying out first small and now increasingly larger Japanese gardens. Gradually a wide range of features has developed which fit well into our western world. These include several whimsically pruned fir trees for the winter scene, as many of the green-leafed Japanese maple bushes, *Acer palmatum*, as possible, Japanese azaleas, camellias, and white or soft pink small-flowered

There are differences between a pool, a pond, and a basin. The first is at the level of groundwater, the second can have an artificial floor, the third always has a watertight artificial floor. This is a basin.

Prunus trees. These are needed to form the roof of the garden; the floor is filled in with stepping-stones, whimsical and flat on top, white gravel, and ground cover. I used all these features in a large Japanese garden in Herlev in Denmark. A client from Belgium went there at my request. She looked round and was convinced that a Japanese garden would be suitable next to the new wing of her house. I was confronted here with a sharply sloping piece of land, which made it possible to work with two waterfalls. Behind the house, next to a large freestone terrace, I put a long meandering pond, which was fed by a waterfall situated slightly higher up. Behind this is a platform and I expect a Japanese teahouse will appear here at some stage. The waterfall became a real masterpiece of ingenuity, because, though we were able to find some marvellous stones, we had to make the whole thing watertight without any of the plastic that we used being visible. It took a lot of effort, but it was successful thanks to the help of professional gardeners.

Now the water gushes via the waterfall into the large lower pond. The water is pumped into a basin which has been made behind the waterfall. The large stones along the edge of the waterfall also serve as stepping-stones, so an element of excitement is added: you can walk where the water falls. This emanates from nature too, where the stones which hold back the water to cause the waterfall are often used by people as stepping-stones.

In the garden of Villa Marlia, which belongs to Count Pecci-Blunt, this formal pond escaped the landscape changes which Elisa Bonaparte, then ruler of Lucca, wanted to carry out. The tall hedges and the fountain make this a cathedral of garden art.

A second waterfall Next to the freestone terrace directly behind the new wing of the house a sunken area has been laid out to save an old nut tree. This provided the motive to install a waterfall here too, this time not in a natural shape, but specifically as an architectural element, by drawing the wall which supports the terrace into the garden and letting the water of the large pond fall over it. It ended up in a low-lying pond, which is surrounded by gravel.

You can hardly carry out a plan like this on your own, unless you have strong neighbours or members of the family, who will help to move the stones. Do not strain yourself – if the stones are too heavy, use a flagstone slab. This is flat and makes a good waterfall, certainly in smaller gardens. Surround these areas, the waterfall and the edge of the pond, with peaceful evergreens such as *Pachysandra* and *Vinca*, and ferns such as *Polystichum setiferum* which remains green in winter, and the problem of integration will solve itself. Be careful with white boulders and do not use too many stones. It is all right to have them, but in moderation. After all, in nature everything soon becomes overgrown, so let the area of the waterfall in your garden be green too, with soft plants, such as a small willow and ferns, and in the water plant the Japanese iris, *Iris kaempferi*, which flowers in dark blue, white, or a combination of the two.

Water pieces are works of art in Italian gardens. The water is often given an imposing source; here in Villa Marlia it flows out of jugs which two reclining river gods are holding.

Wooden, stone, and grass steps

The small gardens of newly-built houses are mostly of flat design. Why avoid different levels?

Seemingly insoluble problems such as prams, wheelchairs, and elderly people who are unsteady on their feet, are used as excuses to avoid having different levels in the garden. These are not watertight arguments, since a step of 15cm (6in) does not present any problem for most prams and elderly people. So I usually become rather energetic if the owners of a flat garden wish for excitement and surprise. I build steps, each of the same height, so that people know how far they need to step up or down without looking. For this is a golden rule: never vary the height of steps from one to another, as this can be highly dangerous and may cause people to stumble.

If you want to enjoy steps when you are sitting in the house looking out into the garden, you must work with increasing heights as you go further into the garden. Then you will see the steps; you cannot see descending steps from inside the room. Depending on the design of the garden you can have a formal flight of steps, which is identical on both sides, or otherwise an informal design with an asymmetrical division of the steps. This is a fairly major decision which you really must make beforehand.

The finest flights of steps are found in the gardens of old Italian villas and palaces. Their consummate shape is modest, yet strong and convincing. Steps, pedestal, statue, and the edge of the pond are all in the same material: freestone, which is covered in grey moss. A lesson in simplicity, however rich the result.

An informal garden design with steps: asymmetry

·With asymmetrical façades, where the door is not in the centre of the rear elevation with an equal number of windows to left and right, there is really no reason to introduce a formal, symmetrical

garden design. It would be better to take the asymmetry of the rear elevation as your starting point and devise a fanciful division of the garden which adopts the interesting features of the elevation. That is what I mean by asymmetrical; the steps are then, as it were, pushed into the plants and the bank, so that the sides are masked. This can be done by covering wooden or stone steps with earth at the ends and putting plants with wide-spreading leaves beside them. You can use an ornamental grass like *Pennisetum alopecuroides*, or a short conifer such as *Taxus baccata* 'Repandens', which spreads out to a great width but remains short (for the first fifteen years, anyway). You could also have perennials such as *Bergenia*, the evergreen elephant's ear, and the deciduous *Hosta*.

Let ascending steps lead somewhere, at least if there is room. This could be a summer-house or a large terrace with a pergola, or a path which winds its way through the plants. Freestone slabs are splendid but heavy, not something to lift and easily lay yourself; you will need help with these. If you do decide on these natural stones it is worth giving some thought to the colour grey. Grey stones do not fit in everywhere, certainly not with an ultra-modern house. You would then be better off having black wooden steps, for instance, or steps which are made out of the same sort of bricks as the house. For a white house choose very dark manganese stones or black concrete bricks.

English architects like Edwin Lutyens were the first to renew the high profile of architecture in the garden. Steps, pergolas, ponds, and summer-houses once again linked the house with the garden.

A flight of steps made of paving stones

Grey paving stones are usually made in the size 30 x 30cm (12 x 12in), but a 50 x 50cm (20 x 20in) format is also available. I designed a round shape for the terrace and pond at the back of a very fine modern house in Vogelenzang, designed by the architect Cees Dam. The house lay in a hollow behind the edge of a dune lined with beeches. To get from the public road to the front door you had to cross the edge of the dune. I solved this problem by taking 50 x 50cm (20 x 20in) paving stones and by first digging them 45cm (18in) upright into the ground. Behind each paving stone I put some cement, which held it in place. The space behind was filled with sand and a second 50 x 50cm (20 x 20in) stone was laid on top. The sides were also strengthened with upright stones, so that the sand could not escape from underneath the horizontal stone. This is the simplest solution for laying a flight of steps and now, after eight years, everything is still perfectly in place.

A naked figure rises from a basin after a refreshing bath, introducing magic and gaiety into this rich combination of walls and steps and a large summer-house with yellow ochre pillars.

Concrete steps

There are many good concrete products on the market which can be used as terrace steps. I once made a staircase by dropping thick, grey concrete kerb-stones upright into narrow dug-out grooves; 30cm (12in) disappeared into the ground and 15cm (6in) stuck out above. I grew box on the grey rim of the tread. On top of the concrete step I put a layer of bricks, which were stuck on with special glue, which still holds after rain and frost and lots of use of wheelbarrows.

If you want something frivolous U-shaped concrete blocks could be the answer. In my Amsterdam town garden I have stood these with both sides touching the ground, so that the top functions as a bench which is never susceptible to weathering. If you put the U-shaped blocks on their sides they become steps. You put one of these blocks on the ground on its side and push the middle surface up to the place where you want a step. The third leg or the third surface becomes the step. These blocks are 40 x 40 x 40cm (16 x 16 x 16in), which is too tall for a step, so you must dig in the horizontal block to a depth of 30cm (12in). A short vertical foot sticks out above the ground and a large 40 x 40cm (16 x 16in) flat slab of concrete forms the step.

With a certain amount of imagination, concrete blocks can be used quite successfully for steps and boundary walls. I did this in a back garden which is slightly larger than standard proportions. However, it is not a really huge garden, which meant that we could lay it out intensively with quite expensive concrete blocks.

I made the front part of the garden level with the floor of the living-room and piled up the dug-out earth onto the area behind, which was already at a slightly higher level. At the border, which was at approximately two thirds of the height of the garden, I put a little wall of concrete U-shaped blocks. These serve as seats and boundary wall. There are buddleia bushes next to them and lots of creeping plants.

A tree as a monument-cum-sculpture is rightly placed on its dais here, with subtly designed steps and low wall.

Square terraces, which vary in size and overlap one another, run from the house through the garden, from the living-room to the large terrace next to the boundary wall of concrete blocks. They are used here with the middle surface standing vertical, therefore in front, and the two feet pushed into the earth bank which lies behind them. So it becomes a 40cm (16in) high wall with a seating edge with a depth of 40cm (16in). This garden became more distinct because of its large hook-shape. Low steps, each 15cm (6in) high, lie between the square small and large terraces. The owners are great lovers of rock plants, so the area has been lavishly strewn with these to provide growth over the hard edges of the mathematical shapes. Right at the back of the garden I put a shady terrace with a pergola, from which there was a grand view over the lower garden. Behind the hedge was the compost heap, which had to go somewhere. A large collection of *Fuchsia* in pots cheers up the garden in places which are sometimes colourless, since rock plants mostly flower in the spring. But I introduced a lot of other long-flowering perennials. A simple, labour-intensive structure for a boundary wall has resulted here in a modern solution. A brick boundary wall is much more expensive *and* much more common.

Wooden flights of steps

If you are considering wooden steps, you will be all right with various types of wood which come from Africa, such as iroko, or from Indonesia, such as teak. There are many sorts of hardwood on the market which are sometimes cultivated in plantations. This seems to be the case with a lot of Indonesian teak. Even so, it is also a good idea to look for alternative materials for wooden steps.

Green wood is a material which has been hardened under high pressure with a chemical. This is how it gets its green colour. This guarantees that it will last for ten years in contact with damp earth. Buy the wood from a firm with a good reputation, whom you can consult if the wood starts to rot sooner and, if necessary, if you are in doubt, ask for a certificate of guarantee.

To construct wooden steps hammer small square wooden posts at least 50cm (20in) into the ground, and 15cm (6in) below the steps; nail one, two, or three boards, depending on their width, onto them above the lowest level. One step is 15cm (6in) high, so two boards are sufficient. Make sure that at least 10cm (4in) of the board is in the ground to prevent the earth being washed away. You can then cover this with another board as a tread, if you like, by screwing or nailing a horizontal board onto the square board. If you do not want to do this, you can use, for example, gravel, shells, bricks, or cobblestones on top of the steps; you must then keep the square foundation poles as deep as possible so that they cannot be seen. If you use a board for the tread, make the top of the square posts level with the top of the tread board, which then stands vertical. This is the simplest, but nevertheless a splendid method of making wooden steps.

Opposite: Descending steps formed with chunks of freestone. The short plants give a sense of space, particularly emphasized by the contrast with the thick bushes.

You can vary this. I often use squares as the basis for a fanciful flight of steps, which may be covered with clinkers or completely with wood. The wood can be stained and naturally you can use oak or hardwood, for example, instead of pine. It would be good if more oak were used; it lasts for a good ten years and goes a beautiful shade of grey, as long as the air is clean.

Stone steps   I could talk at length on this subject. For instance, I could tell you about the pretty steps designed by the English architect, Edwin Lutyens, who devoted a lot of time and work to them. All the paving stones were drawn in great detail, with clinkers as ornamentation or sometimes with very unusual round and semicircular shapes for the treads. If you want to see these at their best you should go and see the garden at Great Dixter in southern England. Here you can see one of these Lutyens flights of steps, with little round-shaped patches of grass and round and semicircular steps of natural stone. It must have cost a fortune to build, but now, after more than sixty years it is still an important part of this garden.

In an average back or front garden these shapes would look out of place and be too overwhelming. This is why steps are made of bricks, and have foundations of 60cm (24in) to prevent them cracking in the frost. The ground behind and underneath the step moves in the winter when the water in the earth expands. This pressure can cause

This regal flight of steps is very inviting. Take note of the overhanging freestone edges, the splendid blending of the steps with the walls, and especially the incredibly fine hedges which surround the entrance gate to the next garden. The steps here become an art-form.

whole walls to burst and crack. A disadvantage is that a lot of money is going into the ground as foundation, but if something lasts a long time and stays in good condition, you tend to forget that. The price is certainly an important factor, so consider carefully whether it really would look best to make a flight of steps from clinkers, possibly combined with a wall seat, a pond, or other feature.

Small freestone walls

Though often used in the past, stone walls have become increasingly rare because of their high cost. But I think a revival is coming, as I have noticed that increasingly these straight slabs of natural stone are being used for low walls and steps. This material must stand on a foundation layer, a layer of dug-in paving stones, for example, onto which the slabs of stone are fixed with cement. You can also make a low dry-stone wall and let the steps slope backwards slightly, though not too much, because that makes them difficult to walk down. Laying them at an angle is important for resisting the pressure of the earth when it is frosted or damp. A wall with stones stacked directly on top of one another would be pushed over easily. Choose natural stone in grey or reddish tints and plant ferns and *Campanula* in between.
Grass steps work only if they are wide and are not walked on too much. This is why a large paving stone or some cobble-stones are put on a patch like this. If you have grass in your garden it looks attractive if you link the front with an area of grass at the back using

Stepping stones can be made of natural stone or of wood, which creates harmony with the wooden terraces.

wooden, stone, or concrete steps, on which grass is used for the treads. This needs to be the same width as your lawnmower.

A garden with grass steps

In my opinion often the best way of linking two sections of garden which are on different levels and are covered in grass is with grass steps. There are various ways of making steps like these. You could consider a step which consists solely of grass, which will look good but is very labour-intensive. You have to cut the front of the steps by hand, which is a tedious job. The tread can be cut with a mower. This is why I usually make a step from a hard material and lay a flat piece of grass on top to form the tread.

In Belgium, in Sint-Truiden, where a flat garden already existed behind a bungalow, a piece of ground was added to the garden, which ran upwards at an incline starting at the level of the new land. Grass steps were made to link the old garden with the new, to emphasize as much as possible that both parts belonged inextricably together. Now there is low-level grass, which was already there, free-stone steps with grass on them, and the grass lawn which leads upwards to various terraces and ponds by means of a walk across the grass or along the paths which have been laid at the sides. So grass is the linking feature in the garden and, like a green carpet, it leads the wanderer on a true voyage of discovery.

Steps and paving here are made of large-headed clinkers which are cheaper than the little clinkers. They are quite appropriate for bigger gardens, but the result can be rather heavy in small gardens. Underneath the steps is a large paving stone, to which the clinkers are fixed with mortar (Huis de Dohm in Heerlen).

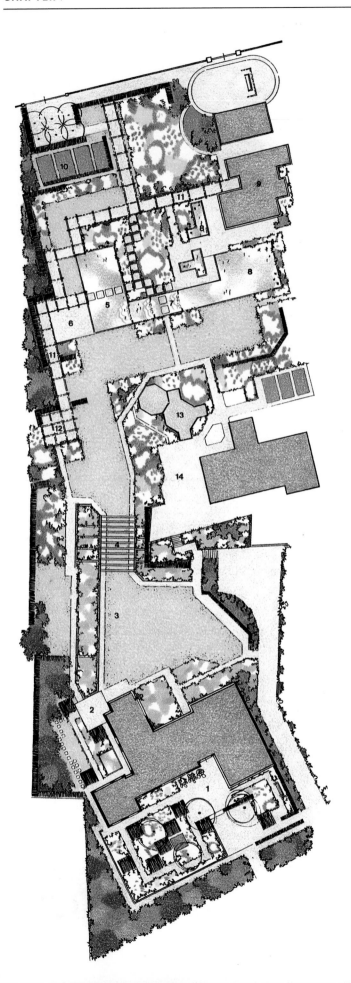

A flight of steps in the garden

In Sint-Truiden in Belgium a large garden was laid out in stages.

1 At the front was a white-flowering garden with squares of yew and a high garden wall. Here there is a statue by Armano, a bronze lady, on the entrance terrace

2 This is a roofed terrace with lots of ornaments and hardwood tables and chairs

3 This became the spacious lawn with plantings of salmon-coloured roses such as R. 'Just Joey', with a view onto 4

4 Broad flight of steps with grass treads leading to the long lawn over which visitors are taken to the new pond (5)

5 New pond, next to which a sunken wooden terrace has been put in

6 Deckchairs and pots with globes of box stand here

7 From this pond the water flows via a waterfall-cum-steps into the pond (5)

8 High level pond, situated in front of the garden house-cum-studio

9 Garden house-cum-studio

10 Here annuals and bulbs are raised for cutting

11 A covered pergola offers a dry walk to the terrace (12), even when it rains

12 Covered terrace where baskets of annuals have been placed

13 In the glasshouse tropical hothouse plants are cultivated and flowers and plants for the house and the studio

14 Large terrace of cobblestones next to the glasshouse

Fencing for shelter and privacy

What is more delightful in the spring and autumn than finding a sunny corner in the shelter of a fence where you can enjoy the sun which, though weak, is nevertheless warming . . .

Fences For me, hedges are the best walls in a garden, so, if at all possible, I plant hedges of box, beech, hornbeam, and holly. These are my favourite hedges. However, there are places where fences are better, for instance in a garden which is still completely bare, where any windbreak is welcome, and they are a welcome change in a surfeit of hedges and brushwood. In any case they can be attractive objects in a garden, as long as they are well made and have sufficient detail.

Black-stained fences of vertical boards, for example, are very striking. Make them "light" structures by fixing the boards with a space between which is slightly narrower than the width of the board. Fix a similar series of alternate boards (i.e. a board opposite a space) at the back, and the result will be light. The construction is simple for anyone who is handy. Take posts of 2.5m (9ft) in length, 80cm (32in) of which is set into the ground. Drill a hole with a soil drill and sink the posts of about 8 x 8 or 10 x 10cm (3 x 3 or 4 x 4in) into it. Hammer them in, so that the tops are all at the same level above the flat ground. Pour some cement round the foot of the post or shovel the dug-out earth round it and tread it in firmly. Fix two cross slats horizontally onto the posts 30cm (12in) from the top and 30cm (12in) from the bottom. The visible boards of the fence are nailed to these cross slats. Everything should be stained, preferably beforehand, black, dark green, or grey. If you do it later it is a tedious job.

This "Jardin d'amour" in Brussels was designed not long ago by the landscape artist René Péchère. It consists of low box hedges and topiary, yew hedges, and annuals in a paving of granite cobble-stones.

A vertical latticework fence

If you like a rather oriental atmosphere you can choose square lattices of about 4 x 4cm (1 1/2 x 1 1/2 in) which are mounted vertically on the side that will be seen. Keep the same space of 4cm (1 1/2 in) open between the slats, then the whole thing will be transparent. Plant honeysuckle, evergreen *Lonicera henryi*, roses, and *Aristolochia* up against it.

Ready-made fences

These are usually made of pine which has been hardened and is slightly greenish, later turning grey. On my balcony I had two of these which consisted of horizontal lattices, which were "woven" around the supports, so that there were tiny cracks, through which I could sometimes just see the tips of my neighbours' feet. I grew as much blue wisteria and honeysuckle as possible to cover the fence with greenery. If you are in a hurry to sit in the open you can get a prefabricated fence at a garden centre or make one yourself. Fix it well to firm square posts, so that it cannot blow over. And do not forget that climbing plants increase the danger of blowing over because their mass offers more resistance to the howling wind. This is why there are cracks between the boards, to let some of the wind through, while the fence still offers shelter from the wind.

Avoid fences with a curve at the top of each section. It makes them unnecessarily romantic and overpowering, while it is almost impossible to disguise this shape with plants when you are fed up with it.

These artistic latticework partitions made of bamboo and rope stand in the Ritsurin Park, a centuries-old garden in Japan.

So keep the top straight. Make sure there is sufficient space behind the fence for evergreen hedge plants such as yew, holly, and privet, then you can always remove the fence. If you want a hedge like this to become really thick on the side next to the fence, there must be a distance of at least 60cm (24in) between fence and hedge to allow enough light to reach the bottom of the hedge.

I think those vertical or horizontal ready-made trellises which you can buy everywhere are exquisite. A lot of fast-growing climbers soon make these thick, so order masses of *Clematis montana*, which is pink in the spring, *Clematis vitalba*, which is white in the summer, and kiwis, which develop large leaves. A trelliswork like this can develop into an object of real beauty.

Protection against intruders: trelliswork on the fence

One side of the garden of my neighbours in Amsterdam is right next to a busy road, where the odd reprobate walks past at night. They have put a trellis on the creamy white-painted fence with a gate, which, after mutual consideration, they chose to close off their garden. On enquiry, it proved to have been put there not only for the sake of its beauty. It is quite a light trellis, which makes an infernal din if an intruder tries to climb over it.

Special trellises

Jan van der Groen, an illustrator, established the seventeenth-century fashion for summer-houses. In his book *The Dutch*

A narrow wall here divides two parts of a garden, which remain visually linked by the windows put into the wall.

Gardener, there are all sorts of designs for trellises. They were often built as a corridor from one garden to another, or they stood as eye-catchers at the end of a garden. These ornamental trellises can be seen in the prints of Het Loo, the palace of William III and Mary, especially in the kitchen garden, which unfortunately has not been restored. They are tall structures, which break up the long walls of espalier apple and, in particular, pear trees, and form elegant monumental gates. Climbers were probably trained between them, but this was not actually necessary. The trelliswork was an ornament in itself, without having to have climbers, which are often rather untidy. You often see them used in Belgium and France and fortunately plenty of attention is being paid to this aspect during the restoration of the palace gardens at Het Loo. Against the brick walls in the sunken "lower garden", a blue-painted masterpiece of a trellis, which has slats going in all sorts of directions, has been brought together in a splendid arch composition. This should be an inspiration to everyone. Yet a lot of garden owners cannot face the work involved in making something like this; it is an unknown art-form of wooden slats and the maintenance of it frightens them off.

Fine trelliswork at Walenburg and in Rekum

Mr Canneman, who was the owner-resident of Walenburg Castle for decades, took with him from his town garden in The Hague a trellis which he had designed and put together. This was placed against a

A trained plum tree forms an attractive fence.

dark part of the south façade. A freestone pedestal was placed in front of it with an ornamental vase on top with a closed lid. The end result was romantic and refined, especially owing to the *Macleaya*, which grew here under the windows, the light blue *Ceanothus* 'Gloire de Versailles', and *Rosa* 'Blush Noisette' with its delicate flowers. When Mr Canneman and his wife, who was a landscape gardener, were asked to design a garden in the Belgian village of Rekum they did it with verve. On the large terrace he put a copy of his own trelliswork, but it was just slightly different. At Walenburg Castle it had a straight top; here a pointed, or rather tympanum, shape was chosen. Both trellises are painted white. The trellis at Walenburg was removed to Leiden. The Netherlands Garden Council, which has taken on responsibility for the Walenburg garden and has opened it to visitors, hopes to bring this work of art back sometime.

A trellis in the garden of an Amsterdam warehouse

Where the house numbering commences on the Keizersgracht in Amsterdam is a row of warehouses which have been converted into dwellings. I helped here with two garden areas. One of them was a normal back garden, which was laid out in two stages. The other is an alley at the side of the canal, next to the warehouses, which is closed off from the road by a large iron door. This door can be opened, leaving room for a couple of cars. The end of the alleyway has been made into a garden with yew hedges and containers of perennials. It is a pleasant garden, which gets the sun in the morning, so it is wonderful to have breakfast there. There are arches of dark green iron embellished by lots of hortensias.

A trellis has been perfectly constructed by a local furniture maker. The colour is light bluey-green, which is surprising. Trellises are usually white, green, or blue, but light sea-green is a novelty. Honeysuckle, kiwi, and hortensia grow up it, and in the middle an espalier pear tree, which was already there growing laboriously upwards, is given a second chance. It can now be fixed in place. After intensive thought and many sketches, we chose as a design for the trellis flat sides and an arch curving downwards so that the whole thing did not look too regal. This proved to be a good contrast with the iron arches which curve upwards. So even a sombre alley with paving stones can be made quite attractive, as long as attention, money, and love are devoted to it.

Simple trelliswork for fruit

If you like espalier fruit trees, choose a trellis to which the branches can be secured while they are still young and flexible. Make the trellis as simple as possible. Put supports in the ground, nail a couple of horizontal beams to them, and to these attach square 4 x 4cm (1 1/2 x 1 1/2 in) strips, which are fixed a reasonable distance apart. This simple pattern of vertical slats makes a tranquil contrast to the irreg-

Facing page: You can let the rush matting used here become completely overgrown or you can wait until a thick hedge or border of shrubs planted behind or in front of it makes the matting superfluous.

ularity of the branches of the fruit trees, which always have short shoots. These are left, because they contain the blossom buds and therefore the future fruits.

Tall garden walls for privacy

In the Deventer Berg district thorough restoration and renovation of a run-down neighbourhood have resulted in an inspiring example of urban renewal. All the gardens and courtyards had walls put round the outside. This way even a courtyard of 4 x 4m (13 x 13ft) became intimate and pleasant and larger gardens were full of atmosphere, partly also owing to the warmly coloured brick walls. You must, of course, have supporting buttresses if you build long walls, otherwise they fall over. A buttress is essentially a square pillar placed on each side of a wall. The buttress is thicker than the wall, and the fixed point from which a structure like this acquires strength. Garden owners do not often build walls, partly because they are expensive, more expensive than hedges. Also, it is often not allowed, even though a fresher breeze is blowing at the moment in the world of planning permission.

If you are determined to have a wall, ask at the council offices and you may be lucky. If a wall like this stands at the boundary with your neighbours you will have to get their permission too. If they are equally enthusiastic about the idea, you may be able to share the cost of building it.

These hedges, like green walls, lead the eye through the gateway in a brick wall to a round topiary form which has been placed in a further gateway as the focal point.

An Italian patio with walls

These days almost everyone goes abroad on holiday and the results are apparent in gardens: terracotta pots, cane chairs, iron benches, bistro tables, French geraniums, *Abutilon*, *Hibiscus*, and oleanders. They are reminders of those wonderful sunny countries, though you can also come away from countries like Norway and Denmark with objects for your own garden.

A number of years ago I was asked by a lady client to fulfil her dream: a Tuscan garden. She would really have liked to live there permanently, but her husband's work and her own activities made this, for the moment, a theme for the future. So to give her a taste of this atmosphere in the coming years, I had to design an Italian garden in a garden behind a newly built house. On one side stood a garage with a brick wall. So there was a wall on the left and I advised building 2.5m (9ft) walls behind and to the right as well. We succeeded with this after discussion with the neighbours. There was a Japanese garden with moss, bonsai, bamboo, and camellias, all of which was removed and I must say this grieved me, but you cannot combine Japan and Italy in a small patio garden. At the end I placed a summer-house of white-painted lattice-work with a pointed roof and a triangular pediment above the entrance. The rear wall was made semicircular to suggest extra space. This curve ended in a round central flower-bed with two semicircular water basins to the left and right of it. Two lions' heads spouting water were fixed to the

I found these baskets, which are carved from the same stone as the window frame, in Portugal. Grey with terracotta proves to be a good colour combination for walls.

walls, all of which were plastered. Then came box, lavender, and old-fashioned roses in apricot and pure white. The floors, the basins, and the benches in the summer-house were made of Haddonstone, a mixture of sandstone chippings and cement with a lovely pale sand colour. The walls were painted in the same colour. At the end were pointed holly bushes pruned into a conical shape. They are 2m (6ft) tall and give sufficient balance in this rather pale garden to a low yew hedge which has been placed against the wall. White-flowering *Wisteria* has been planted and is trained just like climbing roses. It was a challenge to make such a large summer-house in a small garden; the result gives a great feeling of space.

Hedges The hedge I use most consists of *Taxus baccata*. It is strong, hardy, and easy to prune and cut back if it gets too wide or too tall, as the bare branches soon begin to sprout again. It can stand in the half-shade and likes to be relatively dry. Spray it when it has just been planted and if your garden is on dry land. It is not resistant to damp; the roots should not stand in a water-logged area, as they will rot. I discovered this in my garden in Zeeland, where all the yews died in a low, wet spot: they had rotted. Look for a well-drained spot or put in drainage which takes away the ground water. The ground can also be raised enough so that the yew roots do not directly touch the moisture. You make a sort of bank or you can work in some rubble

A pond, a bench, or a garden vase can be a point of tranquillity between tall hedges.

Left: if you want to camouflage an ugly grey concrete wall, an excellent way of doing this is to grow evergreen climbers on it. Espalier lime trees provide extra privacy in the summer in this Amsterdam canal garden.

under the yew hedge. This led to reasonable results at Castle Walenburg. The ground is so marshy that half the garden no longer contains any yew hedges, as they have rotted time after time, though they survive in the slightly higher central part of the garden. Here they are combined with hornbeam, *Carpinus betulus*, and the amazing thing is that this has become one of the charms of this garden. In the winter you can look through the hornbeams, which makes the winter scene transparent and surprising.

Beech: brown in the winter, green in the summer

Beech hedges like well-drained sandy ground which is quite rich in nutrients; after all, farmers would not plant hedges of beech otherwise. These hedges are kept low in front gardens, about 50cm (20in) high, and become taller if the function of the garden space demands it. In the kitchen garden they are 1m (3ft); tall enough to hide the netting which is in the hedge and to keep out hares and rabbits.

Beech hedges are wonderful if you like brown in the winter. If you plant a beech hedge you will have to suffer for the first year, because it takes at least a year before the beech really strikes, at least this is the case on clay. Leave it alone, spray if necessary to prevent drying-out and burning, and wait. The parts that have withered recover and then the miracle occurs: after the first year of sorrow and misery the leaves really begin to sprout and the awaited growth begins.

For optimum security, netting is spread between, behind, and, if necessary, straight along hedges, which then grow through it so that the netting is no longer visible.

Brick is used here for a garden wall. The post supports a white pergola and the hortensias in barrels, which are stored in the barn every winter, are also white.

Privet hedges Privet really is an indestructible hedging plant, which will keep going in a wet, dry, warm, or fairly shady position. I planted a number in an alleyway which was more or less completely running with water and where I needed to put a hedge. The privet is just right, because the roots evidently can stand in the moisture. So if you have a damp garden, think about privet, which can be trained into all sorts of shapes and heights. Cut it at least once a year, preferably twice, then it stays compact. There is one disadvantage: *Ligustrum* is not supplied in large plants, so you have to start with small plants, which are reared gradually. It is no good wanting height too soon, otherwise the hedge is left standing "on bare legs". Let it grow a bit taller each year until after three or four years the hedge is 1.5m (5ft) tall.

If you want quick results choose hornbeam (*Carpinus betulus*), holly, or hawthorn, which is prickly and offers good protection against vandals. There is plenty of choice. Some garden centres exhibit all the possible varieties of hedges. Have a look at these before you spend a lot of money on the wrong choice. Also, see what is successful with your neighbours. Choose a similar hedge for yourself, unless it is laurel, as this is really a very rough hedge with such big, shiny leaves that it becomes difficult to create a gentle atmosphere. Laurel makes gardens look small, and *Prunus laurocerasus* 'Rotundifolia' can be damaged by frost. A good alternative is *P. lusitanica*, with smaller, elongated leaves and excellent growing power.

This wall of browny-beige natural stone has been put up at Hever Castle to provide a background for Lord Astor's collection of Roman and Greek marble statues. They are arranged in a whimsical but splendid composition and linked to each other by a variety of plants.

Left: An old garden wall at Barnsley House separates the garden from a farm track.

More ways of dividing space

Beside hedges, walls, and fences, there are other ways of dividing a largish garden to increase the unexpected. Ironwork is one such possibility.

This has become very popular and is available in all sorts of shapes. For instance, there are obelisks, on which you can grow roses, or, even better, *Clematis*. These often have pyramid shapes, which consist of rods of iron painted dark green, which all come together in a point.

You can get them in different heights or have them made to a particular height by a blacksmith. I discovered that the latter is not cheap, when I had arches put up in my garden.

Iron arches In my garden in Zeeland I have a series of arches where one part of the garden crosses to another. So far, I have not been able to decide what to grow over these arches. Will it be pears, grapevines, holly, or old-fashioned types of rose which will be trained into an arch? I still have time, but eventually I will have to decide. Fortunately I am not always so indecisive, and when it came to a long strip of garden at a house in Vught, I soon decided on the idea of placing arches across the long grass path.

There was to be a blue garden on each side of this strip of grass, so blue plants were placed over the dark green-painted arches, which ran from left to right across the straight grass track. Now this did not prove to be so easy, since there are no blue roses. There is blue *Wisteria sinensis*, and there are blue-coloured grapes and blue-flowering *Clematis* varieties such as *C. alpina* and *C. macropetala*.

Features which seem to appear from nowhere in an open space ... A statue like this Mercury, however white it is, needs some relief if there is an empty space round it. Here Chamaecyparis pisifera *'Plumosa' is pruned into the shape of a large evergreen globe.*

Additionally, the white roses 'Bobbie James' and 'Wedding Day' were planted, which only flower once, but profusely. The wisteria and the *Clematis alpina* are the first to flower, then comes *C. macropetala*, followed a little later by the climbing roses. *Vitis vinifera* 'Rembrandt', the black grape, with its blue-coloured fruit, comes later still. *Vitis vinifera* 'Purpurea' is also fascinating with its dark red foliage. This was planted somewhat later.

The desired result is achieved by the roses which produce long branches, the wisteria with its hanging tendrils, the grapevines with yards of bunches of grapes hanging elegantly downwards: the rather boring blue garden is now a green fairy-tale garden divided into several areas by the curtain of flowers and greenery, which has been created by the arches and the climbing plants.

Magnificent examples of topiary have been created in Longwood Gardens, America. This Taxus baccata *is quite frost resistant.*

Walls with pots A formal way of dividing up a space, but one which lends ambience, is with low brick walls. It is a pre-eminent idea used by landscape gardeners to extend the line of a building into the garden, working with the same material, so that a strong link is established between building and garden. It is important to take as much advantage as possible of these little garden walls and to introduce a difference in the height of the earth on either side of the walls.

Imagine a flat, boring town garden, or the garden of a newly-built house which gradually gets deeper. After the terrace behind the

house and a strip for perennials, roses, or herbs, there are little walls on both sides of the middle area. These, as it were, enclose the view. This view is also the central path, which can be made of grass or stone. Then you go down one or two steps, to a sunken garden, or upwards. I shall begin by imagining that I am going down to the sunken garden.

Garden urns can be strong eye-catchers if they are put on a platform, or plinth. Here there is a border of fruit trees beside the ornamental vase.

The sunken garden

As you descend to the slightly sunken garden, you may discover peace or excitement. You can, for instance, lay a tranquil lawn there, which is fringed with colourful borders, possibly in pinky-purple and blue. This is what I call tranquil excitement. If, after descending the steps, you arrive at a splendid pond, this is spectacular, as long as the pond is well planted and there are also plants beside it which give sufficient balance and are captivating enough to make it an experience.

Maybe you will step into a formal sunken rose or herb garden with little box hedges, or there may be a pleasant square with lots of pots and a large stone table in a corner of this sunken terrace. Reclining chairs and pergolas – anything can go here, as long as there is a feeling of space and surprise.

Introducing a formal design

If your garden is long it is dangerous to put in tall plants or tall objects right at the beginning. This is why sunken gardens which

89

Cypress is the conifer which has taken over the function of Taxus *and* Thuja *in Mediterranean countries. You can let it grow in tall, thin pillars or prune it into hedges, as here at Villa Marlia near Lucca in this Teatro di Verdura (green open-air theatre).*

come after a large terrace are successful. A grandiose example of this is the garden of the palace of Het Loo. Here there is a large flight of steps with pillars, statues, and ornamental vases directly behind the large border at the back of the palace. The steps lead to a sunken garden, which you can easily see from the first floor of the palace and from the border. This is called the "lower garden" and has not been deepened without reason. The owners wanted to have water flowing there, but there was no electricity at that time, and there were no electrically-fed water pumps which could make the water gush to whatever height was required. In the seventeenth century, when the garden of Het Loo was created, natural water pressure was necessary to have water gushing from a fountain. Basins were filled with water from neighbouring streams. These basins were higher than the dug-out lower garden. By linking the two together they were able to create fountains, which were exactly the same height as the water level in the basins. Thus the famous fountains of Het Loo were created, for which the lowering of the garden was essential. Now that electrically-operated pumps exist there is no need to lower the garden.

In a long formal garden which I designed not long ago, I put in a sunken area of garden immediately after the large terrace behind the house, to avoid a long narrow effect. The size was determined by a

This super peacock made of yew has developed over years of pruning.

side wing of the house which protruded slightly beyond the rest. You look out of the house and from the terrace onto the sunken garden, which has been planted with lavender and low rose bushes. In the central part there is a rather elongated water basin with stone edges with a small fountain in it. The rather elongated shape arose from the knowledge that you always see this garden in perspective, in the direction of the length. So rectangular looks square and round oval, while a genuine square shape gives a broader impression, in other words not square. This distortion by perspective is something which all architects and visual artists take account of.

Beyond the pond there is grass, and then a couple of low formal box gardens, at the back of which you can see the grass on a slightly higher level.

A pergola as a space-dividing feature
Because pergolas usually stand on vertical supports or have beams which are fixed between two walls standing opposite each other, they are light objects and you can look under them, as you can with trees. So you could just as easily plant trees, if a pergola is too expensive. But it is not the same, as anyone will agree, because a pergola can have a great number of flowering climbing plants grown on it, and the most trees can do is flower themselves. Blue wisteria, roses with *Clematis*, a multiplicity of rose varieties and soft yellow-flowering honeysuckle, *Lonicera*, can be trained over the beams.

In Valkenswaard I designed a swimming-pool with a sturdy pergola, which also became the roof of the changing cubicles and the shed housing the machinery further up.

Depending on the purpose of the wooden structure, it can be made heavy or light. I like heavy beams myself, so I often have boards screwed to the top of the pillars: two boards on each, and if possible a second layer of boards fixed to them at right angles underneath. Then you get a solid mass of wood, which effectively breaks up the space, especially if it is large, but you can still see under it. You can also cover supports of, for instance, 10 x 10cm (4 x 4in) with strips of wood on top of the supports, which are also 10 x 10cm (4 x 4in) square. This is a good structure if everything is screwed together and the posts are firmly anchored in the ground.

The simplest solution is to pour cement into the hole which the post goes in. This makes it firm, but has two disadvantages. First, it is almost impossible to remove and second, climbers do not grow in concrete, so the plants always have to be planted a little way away from the supports. Therefore the other methods of fixing supports are more interesting.

The Egyptians, Romans, and Muhammadans introduced water as an element of linear perspective. This reflecting pool can be found along the River Vecht.

Pergola supports on a plinth

For years I have had pergola supports placed on a concrete plinth. A hole is left in the tinplate which is buried in the ground. A galvanized iron bar is fixed into this and concrete poured round it. There are two ways of securing the supports to the iron bar. First, you can drill a hole at the bottom of the supports the same size as the iron bar and fix the supports onto the iron bar. This works well if the two

Hedges with trunks, known as espalier trees, emphasize a view or form a wall which visually closes off an area .

fit perfectly together. The second possibility is to put a plate on the iron bar. This plate is the support for the post which is screwed firmly to it. To make it easier to screw it on, the plate is made into a bowl-shape with upturned ends. There are holes in this for the screws, to make it easier to turn the screws into the posts.

One advantage is that this creates a light effect because the post is raised slightly above the earth by the iron bar which stands free of the ground. It gives a rather refined feel to the whole thing. Beyond this, what you choose depends on the garden. If the atmosphere is rustic, with a farmhouse, for instance, you will put the posts, preferably hardwood or hardened pine, in the ground. In the case of a new building or a modern house, choose posts on a bar, and it will look as if the whole thing is floating. These details are certainly important in smallish gardens with newly built houses.

The right place for a pergola

Sometimes there is a rather boring patch of ground behind the house where you would like to introduce more surprise. By planting hedges going from left to right and putting a pergola in the gap left open between the hedges, you can create a new situation full of suspense. A second possibility is to build a pergola further into the garden, where it will be shadowy and mysterious; with a few pots and some nice garden furniture you will soon create a world full of surprises. Or a pergola can be built right behind the house and can

Lorenzo de Medici had grapevines trained over iron arches to create long lines: now it is bare, but in the summer it is a profusion of green foliage and grapes.

serve as a partially covered terrace. If it gets the sun, you can grow grapevines, roses, and blue wisteria over it; if it is in shadow, on the north side of the house for instance, train honeysuckle and *Clematis montana* over it. In a shady spot, with fanciful plants growing right next to the house, you feel as if you are looking from the darkness towards the light. Make sure the pergola does not get too thickly overgrown, otherwise it becomes too dark in the house.

Two pergolas at the side of the house

To keep the view open in long gardens I have two pergolas built at the sides, right opposite each other. This breaks up the length, particularly if they protrude from the side into the middle of the garden. Choose elegant plants with tendrils, such as wisteria and kiwi, which add elegance to these rather solid structures and prevent the appearance from becoming too structural.

Solitary items to break up space

If you do not want pergolas or iron arches there are always plants which are suitable for acting as space-dividers. My creed is: if you can do it with plants, then use them in the first instance and leave out structures as far as possible. Use bushes, for instance, or small trees to break up space.

Well-known plants from the 1960s are stag's-horn sumach (*Rhus typhina*) and angelica tree (*Aralia elata*). You see these so often that people are looking for other plants which are naturally bare at

Perspective is created by arches, by the connecting lines between them, by the long low plant beds full of silvery-grey foliage, and by the ornament towards which the eye is being lured.

the bottom. These days I plant lots of magnolias which have been cut away a bit at the bottom or thinned out, so that you can see under them. Or I use dogwoods from America: the *Cornus florida*, for example, which you can also leave with a trunk. Or you could choose a globe-shape with a trunk, for example a globe of *Chamaecyparis* with a trunk, which I have used many times. The bare trunk is usually about 1.5m (5ft) tall. If you are sitting down you can see under it, and if you are standing up you are looking at a globe-shape.

There is also holly with a trunk as well as globe-acacias, *Robinia pseudoacacia*, known as 'Umbraculifera', and *Catalpas* with trunks, one of which is also naturally globe-shaped. This is the *Catalpa bignonioides* 'Nana', which has large oval, fresh-green leaves. *Catalpa* can, for that matter, be grown as a bush too. They grow large and broad and are suitable for large gardens in which "fancywork" does not fit. In large gardens you must prune the plants in height or width, otherwise you cannot see under them. Pruning must take place in the autumn or the winter, and summer pruning may be necessary if there are so many side-shoots that you find yourself once again sitting looking at a thick bush. There are also many evergreen conifers which you can prune. *Pinus cembra* and *P. parviflora* are trees which have needles, which grow into fanciful shapes on their own and so do not require much pruning.

This delicate pointed arch has a Gothic feel to it and is a relief after all the round shapes.

Apple trees had been planted in this Belgian kitchen garden along the central path and box was planted underneath. They are now full-grown and the hedge has acquired its own beauty with sculptural rounded shapes.

Eating in the garden

If you are absolutely sure which is the ideal place for sitting in the garden, it might be a good idea to have a little wall which you can sit on or put pots of plants on. Your favourite spot can be used in a practical way for all sorts of activities.

In the garden of Powis Castle, in Wales, an impressive, delicately painted bench, which complements the green tints, has been placed on a flawless paving of stone chippings.

You can integrate other features, such as a barbecue, with a wall seat, which you may decide to cover with a row of grey paving stones. You must take account of the prevailing wind direction in your garden and place a permanent barbecue so that the smoke does not blow into your living-room window. The most common prevailing wind direction is from the south-west, but if you live in a town quite different wind directions may be caused by the surrounding buildings, or you may have made a windbreak by planting a tall spinney in the south-west corner.

Another consideration is to think about the people who live next door. If they get the full force of your barbecue smoke every evening this could give rise to a strenuous argument between neighbours. For all these reasons I often recommend a spot at the bottom of the garden for a barbecue.

The best sort, of course, is a portable barbecue, which you can put in a spot out of the wind, where the smoke will not be a nuisance. If, however, you have long dreamed of having a permanent barbecue, you would do best to have it at the bottom of the garden.

A permanent barbecue at the bottom of the garden

If you have room and it will not make the garden too crowded, it is always fascinating to have a sitting area at the bottom of the garden. This can be extended with a wall seat which can also be used for the barbecue. There are two types of barbecue: standing or sitting. If you like to barbecue sitting down, the barbecue and wall can remain low. If you want to stand up and barbecue you must build the wall higher or make a little sunken terrace to stand on so that you can barbecue at the right level. A table is usually 70cm (28in) tall, and this is also the right height for the iron grill that the meat is placed on. If you build a wall with old bricks it can be romantic, or sometimes rather kitschy. However, with a few nice pots, good furniture and a large ecru-coloured parasol, you can create a pleasant atmosphere with a combination of walls made out of old irregular bricks and beams. If you have a new house you can build the barbecue, wall-seats, and steps in the same stone as that of the house. If this stone is very light in colour, however, it is a problem. Then you should choose a darker brick which is neutral and as inconspicuous as possible, and make sure you have cheerful colours and materials to cheer up the sombre colour of the stones. Terracotta pots, for example, with white-flowering busy lizzies are suitable, and so are wooden barrels with water and marsh plants, such as water lilies.

In this private garden planted with fine leafy plants, the chairs and tables are like those often found outside pubs. Unfortunately they are not yet available outside England (Bramdean House, England).

Portable barbecues   These are available nowadays with a hood which can be closed, which is ideal. When it rains it stays dry and you do not have to sit and look at black flecks of ash on the terrace, which then has to be cleaned. Not for nothing are these portable barbecues gradually driving out the permanent ones.

Preferably buy one with a dark coloured hood, then it can be left outside if you want. Avoid the bright red hood, which will immediately influence the colour of plantings.

Accessories for a barbecue

If you want to make your barbecue spot into a permanent feature with walls, benches, and terraces, you will also want to keep the charcoal, a bag of pieces of coal, and the other necessary accessories, such as a poker and sticks of wood easily accessible. You can do this by including a little cupboard with a door at the front, low down in the wall structure. Make sure you have a thick back wall, so that it does not provide a home for spiders. Make the woodwork simple and straight, and make sure you put an inconspicuous knob on the door of the cupboard where you keep all the things you need for a barbecue.

Eating outdoors, a pleasure

I wonder if it is because of all the travelling abroad, especially to Mediterranean countries, that everyone suddenly wants to eat outdoors? Whatever the reason, this involves an awful lot of lugging of plates, jugs of water, and bowls of food which have to be brought from the kitchen. This is, of course, the reason why the dining terrace is usually close to the kitchen. So a lot of thought must be given to such a terrace and its furnishing. Everyone knows the many items of furniture made of synthetic materials and the white wooden garden

Old flagstones with clinkers laid flat to form a terrace at Barnsley House, with sandstone obelisks next to one of the many little avenues which have been created here.

chairs with high backs, which are wonderful to sit in and therefore bought by nearly everyone. The fact that they are very white and take up a lot of room does not seem to bother anyone. I have been looking for alternative terrace furniture for a long time, and fortunately there is plenty of it.

Hardwood tables defy eternity under a pergola over an otherwise open pond-terrace. The splendid garden urns are a subtle ornament.

A clinker terrace with wooden garden furniture

Clinkers, in other words clay-baked stones of 20 x 10 x 5cm (8 x 4 x 2in) have been traditional materials for the garden since days of old, but they must be hard-baked. The colour varies according to the source: some are yellow, while others are bluey-red and shades of purple. This is the most common colour. Old clinkers are very much in vogue, and are therefore expensive and scarce, but so special, because of the variety in their colour, that it is worth saving up for them, certainly if you want to lay the terrace immediately behind the house. After all, you will then be looking at these stones for the whole winter and in the rain. They will always prove fascinating and therefore a suitable material to use close to the house.

If you like things to be rustic, but still like a fairly straight shape for the furniture, you could have wooden furniture based on an English model. The chairs, which are now for sale everywhere, have wide arms and a back which comes up to just above the shoulder blades. This is my greatest complaint about these otherwise splendid models: my shoulder blades always come up against the ridge made by

the top slat where it joins the boards of the rest of the back, which are slightly further back. So I need a cushion in them, which is a nuisance, because I do not always want to be lugging cushions around. Even so they are still my favourites, these heavy armchairs of hardwood from Indonesian nurseries and plantations. In the meantime something has been done about this back and the top board: there is now an improved model which is comfortable to sit in for hours on end, even without cushions.

A bouguet of flowers freshly picked from the garden.

At garden centres and specialist shops you can see countless other chairs, with or without a back. For instance, there is American furniture, which has been inspired by the wooden platforms used in the keels of boats. Square wooden slats are crossed over each other to make a flat top. The result is a kind of draughtboard pattern with quite small spaces in between, about 5cm (2in) square. This idea, taken from the wooden boat platforms, is used for chairs, tables, and even benches. The backs and the seats of the chairs and benches are made in the same way as the tops of the tables. The corners of all the wooden furniture in this series have been slightly rounded off to create a model which is easy on the eye.

A wooden terrace with cane chairs

Wooden terraces have characteristics which make them desirable for many garden owners. Water-lovers rightly discover that nothing reinforces the atmosphere of water as well as a wooden platform

next to a pond. They are like landing stages in yacht harbours and platforms for fishing and you may like to try to create the same atmosphere. You should leave the wood to go grey rather than stain it, and preferably also use hardwood, the same material used for the landing stages. There it is often made anti-slip by grinding joints and grooves in the wood. This way wood does not get slippery so easily. You do not put iron bistro chairs on a square or rectangular platform terrace like this, because the legs fall through the gaps. For platforms you must choose chairs with thicker legs, such as cane chairs. Cane easily lasts for years if it is properly maintained, in other words dipped in clear varnish. This protects it from drying out. Look at the terrace chairs which are left outside in many places for the whole summer, year in, year out. From the many examples, it would be best to choose fairly simple ones for such a sporty platform-terrace. If you like contrast, choose the chairs which come from Thailand. These come in two models: with a straight back, and with a back which curves backwards, which has been made so that if you lean backwards a bit you can watch the dragonflies laying their eggs at the foot of a blade of reed mace, and waterflies which "wander" over the reflecting water surface.

There are also some very cheap chairs which have backs which end below the shoulder blades; these are quite good to sit on beside a sturdy table.

A simple table made of two thick wooden boards is used to display a composition made up of various old garden articles.

Tables

There are wooden tables which have cane wrapped round their legs and a synthetic marble top, which is very practical. I do not think they are very attractive, because the dull marbled plastic does not go with the natural aura of the cane. A commercial terrace, where the tables are used several times a day, has special demands: the table must be easily cleaned and in this case the dull, browny-grey top is acceptable. But fortunately there are alternatives. There are plenty of wooden tables: round, square, elongated, extending, or oval. Choose from these something which is appropriate for the number of people who are going to sit and eat or drink coffee at the table. A wooden table like this is seldom too big, because people like ornaments on tables these days. Terracotta pots with thyme may be placed on them with saucers underneath, globes of box, ivy, storm lanterns; whatever the fashion of the day, and rightly so, because it looks delightful and full of atmosphere. If you put a bunch of flowers on an outside table this should be placed slightly in the background.

Bunches of flowers on out of doors tables

Flowers last much longer in the garden than if they are picked and put in a vase. This is the most important reason for not picking too many from your ornamental garden, unless you have at your disposal a garden designed especially for picking. You can also grow plants which actually need to be picked to be kept in flower. Sweet peas are plants which have to be relieved of their daily burden of flowers to be prevented from going to seed, as the flower production then stops. This is also true of marigolds, which people like to use for short flower arrangements: you pick them so that they do not produce seeds, and keep blooming. A garden with flowers for picking is a good excuse for having the whole house full of flowers. Putting a flower arrangement outside in sun, wind and rain often proves rather disappointing: the flowers die much more quickly than indoors. Just compare a bunch of phlox in a vase indoors and phlox outdoors in the garden: they stand outside for weeks in full bloom, while indoors they are gone within a week. The same is true for delphiniums, *Lysimachia punctata*, and unfortunately a lot of other garden flowers. I speak from experience, since for years I had allotments outside the town where I live. Then you really do have to pick some things in order to bring home something of the invisible atmosphere and to enjoy it for a bit longer.

In England I once saw a splendid example of a way of dealing with flowers from the garden. It was in Sissinghurst, Kent, the ruined castle from the time of Elizabeth I, where Vita Sackville-West lived with her husband Harold Nicolson. She had her own study high up in a rarefied residential-cum-combat tower, which stands like a pillar in the middle of the formally laid out garden. Many who have visited the garden will remember the profusion of plants. This combination has made their garden into the source of inspiration for many others all over the world.

It was a risk putting such a striking red-painted garden bench here in a completely green environment with the dark green ivy as a background, but it looks absolutely right.

Facing page: A slender soft green iron table with chairs against a green background of Virginia creeper.

On Vita's desk there was always a little bunch of flowers from her garden. Sometimes there were several little glass vases filled with flowers. She felt that her garden represented the bunch of flowers and arranged her flowers in the same way. This became the great revolution in planting gardens. Flower arrangements are made up from borders and patio gardens where grey and brightly-coloured foliage are mixed with flowers just as they are in vases.

Wooden furniture on a wooden terrace

The shape of those wooden chairs which were originally placed on the decks of the big ocean steamers, so that the passengers could take the air, is splendid: the sturdy deckchairs, which do not immediately start to slide as soon as there is any swell on the sea. Today they can be adjusted so that you can lounge fully in them or sit more upright. The chairs do not need to be treated, as they are made of hardwood and the colour goes grey.

If you do not want the wood to go grey, but perhaps a bit greenish, you can dip the chairs in oil, which makes them slightly darker. There is then no chance of attack by algae.

Iron furniture on a stone paved terrace

If you are looking for old building materials, you can get them from collectors. They radiate such old age that a terrace made of old, used material is really striking. This is obvious if you look at a paved section of garden where there are worn small-headed bricks, paving

I designed a herb garden paved with clinkers for a property near Staphorst, in which the blue iron table with a parasol, designed by the owner, is the glorious central point.

stones of bluey and dark grey freestone, and other paving stones of sandstone or straight sawn flagstone.

Flagstones come from England; in the Netherlands Weser stone is used, which is precisely the same: stones which are reddish at first and later become pale reddish-beige in the sun and greenish in the shadow. Magnificent terraces can be laid with these, as long as you lay them as a fanciful spot between plants, or as a formal terrace adequately fitted out with good garden furniture. There does not need to be too much of this, but something with allure. Many English country houses have flagstone terraces, on which greying hardwood benches and tables stand. This has become a standard solution: the combination of flagstone with greying furniture, which always looks good. If you want something different you must look for alternatives.

For instance, there is a lot of iron furniture for sale, which is really interesting in shape: tables with scrolled legs, which have no straight lines at all, or tables with legs which are almost semicircular in shape: the top of the half-circle begins underneath the table-top, then half-way underneath the table-top is the middle of the curve, and then it curves out again. There are usually three semicircular legs under a round table-top.

In France they like portable furniture, so there are whole series of folding tables, which are exceptionally practical. Bought new, they

An eye-catcher has been placed in the area normally used for eating: two pyramid plant-stands on the fine hardwood table, with a bench in the same material.

are not expensive. If you often have visitors, buy two or three round or rectangular ones. One is used permanently; the others you put away and get out if there are more people eating or drinking outside. The tables, usually made of iron, have a hole in the middle of the top for a parasol. Put a firm iron pole under the table or plant the parasol in the ground, otherwise the table you have just laid will blow over with the next gust of wind. If you are clever, you will dig an iron pole into the ground for the foot of the parasol to fit into. Or you can keep completely to ironwork and put a special parasol foot of dark green or black painted iron under the table. These are large square chunks of iron with a round foot welded onto them, into which the parasol pole fits. These parasol feet are particularly suitable for the large parasols with a wooden pole. A sturdy parasol foot like this does fit into the standard wooden tables which have a hole in the middle in which there is a little removable disc.

Besides flagstone there is also bluestone, or simply grey freestone paving stones, which are available new or old. Old paving stones are difficult to find, at any rate in large quantities. New paving stones are available in the standard sizes of 40 x 40cm (16 x 16in) and 40 x 20cm (16 x 8in). These are good sizes for making a terrace.

This bench in the garden of the Huis De Doum was previously used as street furniture on an English avenue.

A stone terrace Between Antwerp and Ghent, more or less on the River Schelde, is the village of Berlare, close to Dendermonde. I quite recently

Over-refined benches are better replaced by sturdy sitting areas if you want to combine the three elements of air, water and, in particular, fire for a barbecue.

designed a garden here at a famous restaurant. The garden consisted of grass, with a small dilapidated barn at the bottom. This barn has been restored to a place for largish celebrations. A rather strange construction of gigantic black pillars with a fabric cover stretched across them was used for it, which makes it a nice place to be when it rains and one where you can find shade on warm summer days.

I designed a long pond, which points straight towards the centre of the restaurant. This pond is fed by a basin situated slightly higher up, into which water flows through little stone pipes. This water fills the higher basin, which is linked to the lower long pond by a waterfall. Grey-leafed herbs have been put in around the higher pond, with globes of box and four medlar trees, which are also greyish. The herbs are filmy and fine-leafed, which takes away the hardness of the water basins. Lavender, *Santolina*, southernwoods, and *Artemesia absinthium* stand next to each other here. Round the long low basin a number of large stone terraces have been put in, on which stand slender wooden furniture and parasols. and which are decorated with pots of mint, geraniums with scented leaves, and lots of laurel globes in pots. You could imagine yourself in a courtyard somewhere in France, with the air filled with the scent of herbs. One snag with the paving stones is that they are not easy to clean. To disguise the marks, rub down the stones to create a rough surface.

Following pages: It is not necessary to fill all the pots when using several for a decorative effect.

Garden lighting

Magnificent lamps have been put in the garden of a restaurant. They are vertical posts painted mouse-grey, with a piece of Plexiglass on top, which is cut on the slant.

The lamp is under the Plexiglass cover, which is splendidly lit and directs a sideways stream of light onto the surroundings. I think this is the most attractive modern lamp. My favourite wall lamp is classical and is situated against one of the old walls of my farm. It consists of a frame of dark green painted iron, with glass in it at the front and at both sides. The back is dark green. A cover, with lines which curve towards each other, has been made to go on top of this glass and steel box to house the fitting.

Some striking lamps come from Italy; their presence is sometimes modest, at other times impressive.

Old street lamps, kitsch or classy? When a row of old street-lamps is placed along the drive of a large newly built house in a garden which is still empty, I often find it over-whelming. You should wait until the garden is fully grown with lots of bushes which rustle in the wind and then hide them in between these. They are then more visible in the winter than in the summer. Since I do not really like these nostalgic lamps, I look for alternatives. An example is the simple copper "bull's-eye" storm-lamps, mounted on a square wooden post and sometimes painted dark-green. You can see from the catalogues of firms from various countries that there are certainly some attractive modern lamps. There are also fine Danish aluminium lamps, which can be painted, if you want. Consider carefully and choose something unobtrusive like the "bull's-eye" or a really good "designer" lamp. Poor lighting is annoying and bothersome and can destroy all sophistication, turning an area into something flashy

110

and corny. For years I have bought copies of classical lamps for my clients. But if you have a modern house these do not fit in at all. Get information from good shops and do not restrict yourself to garden centres, even though you can usually find a good and varied selection of lamps there.

Spotlights to highlight an object

Dark gardens appeal to me and I have no lighting in either my town garden or on my farm, except on the outside walls of the house. This can be extremely impractical at times, when you have to walk across slippery paths in the pitch dark, so it is not recommended for everyone. Apart from lighting along important paths, which should be low and pointed downwards, you can choose to light up a tree or bush or even a border with spotlights. If you want to do this really effectively, brute force must be used in the lighting. Large spotlights are placed so that they shine enough light on the chosen object to be able to compete with the light from the room, which is reflected in the windows of your house. Weak spotlights cannot be seen amongst the reflection of reading, table, and wall lamps.

A lantern is often placed on a wall as an ornament. You can see from this designer light from Italy, which goes well with modern buildings, that it does not have to be purely classical.

Place lamps on the edges of paths: they will light both the path and the plants.

There are permanent spotlights, which are fed by underground lighting cables, and there are portable spotlights with cables above the ground. If you want to change them around the latter are good; if you want to light something that will never be moved, then you can have permanent spotlights.

Statues, vases, and other ornaments

Carving statues out of stone or modelling clay into statues or other ornaments is evidently something inherent in human beings. People have been involved in this since the earliest cultures.

This Medici marble vase has rams' heads with large horns. These ornamental objects, which are provided with drainage, can be seen at the castle of Chenonceau on the River Loire.

Likenesses of oxen, warriors, trees from Mesopotamia, and the unimaginably refined Egyptian images of mythical creatures and pharaohs are well known. Mythical creatures and gods, for the pharaoh was also regarded as a deity, played a prominent role at that time when a subject was being portrayed. Even in the present day, people want to portray in stone, bronze, or clay something they feel to be a reality, even though they have not seen it, in tangible proportions. The Greeks made statues of their gods, their philosophers, beautiful women, and also of their worldly rulers, with their generals, chariots, and possibly winged horses. The Romans followed this pattern, though you cannot refer to just one Roman culture. Before Rome was able to leave its mark on the coming centuries as a centre of power and culture, the Etruscan culture which formed the basis of the Roman civilization was already in existence. It was incorporated and, together with Greek influence, made into something new.

Many of the Greek and Roman statues have been copied endlessly. Often the owner of such a copy in bronze, stone, or clay had no idea what the statue represented. It was appreciated purely for its beauty. The opposite, buying statues expressly because of what they represented, occurs later. We know that William III in the Netherlands, just like Louis XIV in Versailles, chose the statues in his garden to symbolize his divine power and importance. Apollo, Narcissus, Galatea, Romulus and Remus, and Arion were ordered by him in mar-

*Iron vases, an
exquisite but
expensive garden
ornament.*

ble or bought ready-made, because of their divine connections and reference to ancient, important cultures.

For many centuries people have occupied themselves with the creation of perspective in the green spectacle of the gardens, and not only with hedges, fine flowers, and water decorations, but in particular by placing significant ornaments in important positions.

Gods and goddesses in a modern-day garden

If you want to avoid a pretentious atmosphere you should deal fairly casually with statues. Put them among hortensias, let clematis twirl around them, give ivy a free hand to wrap itself around the plinth. Tall grey *Artemesia absinthium* will look splendid with them. *Acanthus spinosus* is just right, as a Greek wild plant with its large deeply incized leaves. Above all do not position the statue centrally on a sight axis, but asymmetrically, to emphasize the coincidental in such an ornament.

An asymmetrically positioned statue in Sissinghurst

The white garden of this romantic castle in Kent is portrayed in many gardening books. There are box hedges and clinker paths, and in the centre stands an iron summer-house, whose sole purpose is to support a white climbing rose. This climbing rose is such a fascinating spectacle that you forget everything around or underneath it. This part of the garden is bordered on three sides by a wall, and a tall yew hedge was planted later on one side.

In front of the wall on the north side of the garden is a bush with lots of perennials grouped around it. This bush has grey leaves; it is the ornamental pear, *Pyrus salicifolia*. There are two versions of this: the slightly hanging *Pyrus salicifolia* 'Pendula' and the more perpendicular form with the same name but without 'Pendula' after it. In front of the hanging version of this white-flowering bush, which produces small inedible green pears, is a statue of a young rather withdrawn woman. She is naked and her eyes are meekly looking downwards. The branches of the ornamental pear hang over her shoulders, and spread out like a parasol over her head. A world of sophistication and subtle delicacy is created by the plant, which takes away all the black of the stone. This is the most splendid way to see important and valuable statues: integrated into the garden.

A ball of peat-iron adds a special cachet to any garden.

Modern statues Not long ago I made a new sight axis in a garden in Belgium, diagonally across a number of sections of garden. At the end of this sight axis was a rose garden full of perennials. This garden, which had grass in front of it, is now symmetrically divided into four sections by box hedges. In the middle stands a freestone water sculpture, which was specially designed for this spot by the sculptor, Dekkers. It was a tall abstract statue with a rough surface, which got slightly narrower in step-fashion towards the top. Water flows over it. In the evening the sculpture is illuminated, which is attractive, because you have a full view of it both from the house and from the dining terrace which lies between the statue and the house.

A water pillar Not long ago I designed a water pillar, a tall pillar of freestone, from the top of which water flows downwards. The pillar is straight in shape and fits well into smaller spaces, where statues would make it too crowded and demand too much attention. Sometimes an emphasis is needed, but not a historical statue; this is why I designed a water pillar. The water comes out of the top of the pillar via a small pipe and then flows downwards through little chutes. These chutes are in fact just the sides of the water pillar, which have been shaved away a bit on the upper edge. The pillar gets wet and the water flows and ensures a green sheen on the sides.

Flat dishes with flowing water In Japan many gardens have magic stones onto which water drips via a little bamboo pipe. These stones sometimes have a hollow where water collects. Every Japanese tea-house has a vessel like this by the entrance with water in it, which is renewed daily. If the water starts to look green, fresh water is put in. Everyone who goes into the little building where the tea ceremony takes place "cleanses" himself more or less symbolically, by moistening his hands and face with water from the vessel. There is a little bowl here for this purpose, which is usually made of a piece of bamboo pipe. The hollow in these stones is

This dog keeps guard in the garden of Pashley Manor.

usually quite shallow, so that you do not have to bend over very far to scoop up the water. Some of these have become true jewels of sculpture in stone. Often there is a lantern beside them, made of the same sort of stone, so that you can find the water basin even in the dark.

New and old millstones My grandfather owned windmills. Could this be the reason I am fascinated by flat millstones over which water flows? At one time you could buy these round flat stones with grooves hacked into the surface. In the mill the grain was thrown onto a stone like this, while another stone turned, and ground the grain on it into fine flour. When mills no longer operated because it could be done more cheaply in a flour factory with electrically driven milling machines, the mills were used for different purposes. The stones, which were in the way, were put outside, where they were left, unused and redundant, as a reminder of days long gone. Then suddenly they were discovered and used as ornaments, probably first becoming popular in the Netherlands, a country famous for its numerous windmills.

The stones were put on pebbles amongst ferns, *Hosta*, and hogweed *(Heracleum mantegazzianum)* and water was made to flow through the hole which had originally been cut for the pole, which was moved by the sails of the mill. The water was allowed to trickle away between the pebbles. The next step was to have the water pumped by electrically driven pumps.

The dark stone plinth of this sundial is incorporated into a sophisticated border of white Rosa *'Schneewittchen', which takes away any stiffness.*

116

A concrete millstone

I realized that the millstones would soon disappear if we landscape gardeners continued to recommend them as water features in gardens. Therefore I decided to make a millstone myself, which could act as an alternative. If you go to the Mien Ruys Garden Foundation in Dedemsvaart, you can see my design in the shape of a grey concrete, slightly hollow stone, in which a layer of water can stand. It is filled with water via the central hole in the middle, out of which water flows. The water then falls over the sides down into a layer of gravel. Under the layer of gravel is a tank with a pump in it, which pumps the falling water back up again.

Vases of iron, stone and terracotta

In the nineteenth century and earlier iron garden vases were often placed empty on top of the pillars of a wall or fencing. They were purely ornamental objects, which were intended to give either a delicate feel, or one of bulk, to the structural sections of the garden. The vases were painted black or dark green. They were not usually left unpainted, as rust was not yet "in" as a colour at that time.

In Zeeland, in the southern part of Zuid-Beveland, there is a garden which still has these ornamental iron vases on the walls. In the village of Ellewoutsdijk on the Westerschelde dyke the owner has created a wonderful palace with statue galleries in separate buildings, numerous iron ornamental vases on concrete plinths as features in the garden, and large festive white bridges over rivers which he has had dug.

Two ornaments, one living and one made of stone, both fascinating in shape.

117

Wooden barrels and white wooden containers stand along the stone path. A small avenue has been formed between the containers, crowned with the row of rose arches.

The main house disappeared in the last war, destroyed by an Allied bomb, which was aimed at the house which had been taken over by the Germans. The garden ornaments which were further away from the house were later reinstated as far as possible, and two white villas were built, one on each side of the public road, each one of which contains half the collection of garden treasures. The iron vases in this garden, like their plinths, are painted white. They do not look conspicuous, any more than the other iron statues, of larger than life size ladies blowing ceremonial trumpets, which have been put up at the entrance to the centre of the village.

Fortunately a lot of money and attention has been devoted by the owners of the two new villas to the restoration of these iron ornaments, and the ornamental vases are magnificently preserved and have been provided with new plinths.

Iron vases are now used here and there in the garden as ornamental objects. They are often seen on tables as a composition with ivy in them, or a ball of peat-moss or genuine woodland moss sticking out of them in a tuft. A crystal ball in them is also an attractive decoration. Fir cones, glass marbles, ornamental fruit, etc., can be put in them, or flowers, which you must first put into an inner vase, since most iron vases have a drainage hole.

If you like a rust colour, let them weather to a brownish colour without any fear that they will rust away, as that takes generations. If you like things neat and tidy, paint them dark green, mauve, blue, white, black, or yellow-ochre, whatever goes with your flowers and your house. At exhibitions where old garden furniture and ornamental vases are offered for sale you can see that there are various models: wide, narrow, and short for flower arrangements in the house, or wide, round vases with a wavy edge which curls outwards.

It is difficult to tell with a vase like this whether it was cast last year or a hundred years ago. Be cautious about assurances that you are dealing with old specimens. If necessary, ask for a certificate of age, especially if a dealer is asking for a lot of money and trying very hard to convince you that the iron object is an antique.

The world-famous Medici vases

The so-called Medici vase is clog-shaped. In other words, there is a foot with a neck onto which the vase, which may be in the shape of a calyx or an upside down bell, is cast, with ridges on the side. This model has been copied from the marble ornamental vases which you can see in Italy at the palace of Maria de Medici. There are also some in Paris, in the Jardin de Luxembourg. These vases made of marble were several feet tall, at least if you include the plinth, and, owing to their perpendicular shape, they were unusually elegant for their time. This successful specimen from antiquity has been imitated *ad nauseam* by manufacturers of iron vases, sometimes in authentic proportions, sometimes adapted more to the taste of the day. I must confess that I do become somewhat tired of these

Facing page: Go and look at collections of old building materials and pick out what will fit into your ambience. It is not cheap, but it does save you having to make many trips to search for suitable ornaments.

Medici models and I much prefer the wider vases which can be splendidly decorated.

Terracotta for pots and ornamental vases

Terracotta is a popular material at the moment, which is worked into lots of shapes, particularly in Italy. It is a natural clay from which roof tiles, bricks, and pots are made. Pots from Italy were already famous in the seventeenth century. The clay was pressed into moulds, so that any motifs would show up well when the pots were fired. William III had pots brought from Italy for his gardens at Het Loo, and copies have been made there for the restoration. There are various models, but nearly all of them are narrow at the bottom and wider at the top. This was probably to allow for the expansion of the ground in winter, when the moisture in the earth expands. By having a conical shape to the pots, the earth can find a way out: upwards, led this way by the sloping walls of the pot. Unfortunately many pots have broken because this does not always work. Hence my solution: always put a plastic pot inside the terracotta pot. The earth can then expand in the plastic pot and the terracotta pot is not in danger. This applies only to pots with plants which can be left outside in the winter. Annuals are thrown away or kept in the glass-house; the old earth from the pot is put on the compost heap and the mixed-up compost is used again the following year with some manure or bonemeal. Besides the terracotta pots from Italy, there are also

At the museum of Huis van Loon in Amsterdam a fine, classically painted sundial with lots of gold, and blue and white strips for the hours, stands in the rose collection, which is surrounded by hedges of box.

At Castle Wylre in Limburg a number of modern sculptures has been erected; the amount of space, which quite rightly has been given to them, is breath-taking. The garden is open to the public in the summer and at weekends.

examples from America, which are straight and square and come in several heights. Square containers and shapes which stand tall and upright are very suitable if you want architectural shapes. There are some splendid pots from Greece too, but these have thinner walls than the Italian ones. Their colour is unusual, pale sand-coloured, which is good for delicate-flowering pot plants and looks splendid with green leaves.

I prefer pots with scarcely any decoration myself: just ridges at the top and possibly another ridge in the middle. However, if you set out a collection of those pots decorated with garlands, apples, pomegranates, and lemons, they do have some appeal, as long as the planting is very simple, or otherwise really exuberant.

For me a simple planting is with one variety of the famous *Hosta*, either with blue or with green and white leaves. Choose a combination of a tall plant like the standard marguerite daisy with white busy lizzies, white ornamental tobacco plants, grey foliage plants, white trailing geraniums, and white lobelia.

A surprise, such a modern type of garden ornament. An object like this can fit in with both old and new buildings, as long as you have the space.

Wooden pots and containers

Short wooden barrels with iron rings are very popular in England. The wooden staves are painted white or dark green and the rings white or black. Into these go plants grown from bulbs and annuals, or box with ivy. You see these combined with aluminium hanging baskets, which are filled with trailing plants. Planting in these wooden

One of Giacometti's famous slim figures, photographed here in the Musée Maegth in St Paul de Vence.

barrels always seems to rot them quite quickly, but you can do something about this. Line the walls of the barrel with polyester, so that the moisture does not touch the wood. You can also put plastic inside before the earth goes in, but this does not really help, as the wood still does not stay dry, because although the plastic provides an air-tight seal, moisture still gets in underneath the plastic. But it does help the barrels to last longer.

Trapeze-shaped wooden containers

Sometimes a completely new shape arises out of nothing, such as the wooden container which is narrow at the bottom and gets wider nearer the top. It is a fine container, which can be used in many ways: on each side of a front door, for instance, or next to the door of a terrace. Stand three of them next to a bench, and one with a largish plant in it on the other side of the bench. If you have a dark blue painted bench, a wooden container in the same colour looks nice next to it, even if it does not have anything in particular in it. Globes of yew look splendid in these containers. Choose a container in a grey-blue colour and put grey-leafed plants in it, such as sage, *Santolina*, and *Artemesia*, and to give height, the grey *Pyrus salicifolia*. Yours is the choice of colour: light grey, pale green or perhaps beige, if you like Tuscan colours.

Wooden orangery containers

For centuries wooden containers have been made, in which pine-apple and lemon trees were planted; these were taken inside when

Fortunately copies of all sorts of attractive ornaments are being reproduced, based on old examples, like this one of a dog. It is well integrated into the greenery of Hosta *and hornbeam.*

frost threatened, and were brought outside again when the frost was over. Iron braces were fixed to the sides of the barrels, through which sturdy sticks were pushed so that they could be carried. One man in front and one man behind lifted a container like this onto a flat cart, pulled by an ox, horse, or mule, which brought the fully laden cart to the orangery or the frost-free barn with windows. Now there are fork-lift trucks, which push a steel slide under the containers, which have feet, and lift them on to a cart. The largest orangeries were built in the seventeenth century in the gardens of Louis XIV at Versailles, for the orangery plants from the garden of the Sun King. You can see these impressive buildings from a terrace. In the summer the wooden containers stand outside with palms, pomegranates, oranges, and bougainvilleas in them, and in the winter they are brought inside. In the summer, banquets, festivals, and concerts are given for important foreign guests, and the French tricolour recurs in all sorts of shapes.

At the palace of Het Loo there is also a fine collection of orangery plants, which have been put into round and square wooden containers. Sometimes they are white, sometimes dark green. There is a large orangery here too, to protect the collection when it gets cold. Good orangery containers are well-made, generously proportioned, and made of teak. You can paint teak, so here too the colours green, white, or blue are used.

This antique lead statue ought to be reproduced again as a spout for a fountain. The shell at its foot indicates such a function.

When I once rented a part of the villa Monte Gufoni situated near Florence, this was the first thing I saw in the morning: a stone dog, which watches over the formal garden, where there were both cypresses (symbol of death) and almond trees (symbol of life).

Parasols

You see them on Mediterranean plazas: the enormous parasols which give shade to the visitors sitting on the terraces drinking coffee and wine. And you see them appearing more and more often in other countries too, in gardens and on terraces.

They are wide, to allow as many guests as possible to enjoy the shade. A certain amount of adjustment is required to enable these parasols to be used in gardens in northern parts of Europe too. For instance, you can have a cover with them, so you can protect the parasol when it rains. These covers are supplied in the same colours as the parasols, white or creamy-white.

The splendid thing about the Italian parasols is that they have a pole and a frame, so when you are sitting under them you are looking at wooden slats.

If you visit markets in Mediterranean countries, you will enjoy the large parasols which are used to protect the market wares from sun and sometimes from rain. A sombre square becomes cheerful when these large white parasols are put up with wooden trestle tables underneath them, on which the salespeople spread out their produce and market wares.

A terrace does not look too big if it is well paved with old clinkers. Give it an intimate feel with a parasol, like this Italian wooden parasol which stands on a movable steel plate with an upright holder.

Coloured parasols Large parasols are attractive not only in white or ecru, but also in other colours, for example dark green, deep red, and blue; they are even available in yellow, which is sometimes a good solution if white would be too conspicuous. In a field with lavender, hyssop, delphiniums, and monkshood, in a meadow with wild bluebells, or in a meadow with blue-flowering speedwell, a blue parasol would be much more suitable than one of those white parasols which are seen everywhere. A browny-red parasol is appropriate next to a hedge of red rose hips with a tuft of purple *Eupatorium*, as it also is with all grey tints.

I would not be so eager to choose yellow parasols, but if you have an old farmhouse or town-house with yellow-ochre walls, this is an interesting colour, which looks good with lots of greenery such as holly and fruit trees which have blossom and fruit. If you choose a light coloured parasol, it is best to have one which is relatively easy to keep clean. On a smooth plain surface you can see every little spot. A parasol with coloured panels disguises stains from fallen leaves or berries.

A parasol on the back of a chair

There are also lighter parasols of aluminium. They have a movable foot and you can place the sunshade wherever the table and chairs are. You cannot do this with the wooden shades which stay fixed in one place.

As everyone knows, the sun changes position, so a movable parasol is handy. The question of shade can also be solved in another way, as a painter of gossamer-fine flowers once demonstrated. She often sits in her garden for hours looking at a flower. Then even the straw hat which she wears is not sufficient. A little parasol fixed on to the back of her chair with a short handle and a screw is both adequate and practical.

At an old farmhouse I designed a spacious terrace next to the kitchen, with several containers round it for herbs. On the left you can see the wall of plaited willow branches, which separates the garden from the public road. The parasol stands in the extra large table which has been painted blue.

Unusual paving

One of the most
important ways of
decorating the garden is
with a good, sometimes
even rather unusual
paving. If possible, do not be too
economical with it: paths and terraces last
for years and years.

First of all, think about what the areas to be paved are going to be
used for. For a terrace, on which chairs, tables, lamps, and containers of water are going to be put, the paving can be simple and provide either a cool or a warm base for this abundance of objects. I
shall start with a cool terrace.

I made one of these in a garden by using elongated 40 x 60cm (16 x
24in) grey concrete paving stones, on which a continually changing
arrangement of cane furniture, wooden tables, parasols, and pots
with box shapes was displayed. The simplicity of the paving has
a positive effect here, because there are so many splendid things
which would soon be too much on a fancy paving – the paving thus
makes a restful background.

You can achieve the same effect with small-headed grey stones,
which are usually fairly uniform in colour, at least if you use a stone
like basalt for these cobble-stones. This type of stone has a uniform
grey colour which forms a restful base. The irregularity of the cobble-stones, which are more or less square, means that the effect is
busy enough, even if you do not put a lot of furniture on a square of
paving like this.

I recently had all the terraces around an ultra-modern white-painted
house with a lot of glass paved with cobble-stones: small-headed
basalt stones. The contrast with the rough cobble-stones is fascinating, and gives just the depth which is desired here. Paving stones of

*Rounded pebbles
found in river-beds
and then bedded
according to colour
into loam, clay and
later cement. You can
still see these in old
gardens around the
Mediterranean. Why
is this not copied in
other countries, which
have just as many
pebbles in their rivers?
The result would be
dazzling.*

blue stone, which is in reality grey, were used for the paths in Walenburg, which is open to the public, and also for a restaurant near Antwerp.

In both gardens I laid them haphazardly, in other words they were staggered, to make the whole thing look unmeasured and irrational.

In large gardens, though, a clearly defined spot is often what is desired, as a sort of safe refuge, and then it is better to work with block patterns with straight lines, for example four large stones together with a border of cobbles or bricks around them.

Pavement stones I have gradually gained a great deal of experience with pavement stones, because paving is often one of the most expensive items when laying out new gardens, and often even far exceeds the cost of the new plants which have to be bought. Nevertheless, it is important not to be too economical with the material, particularly with larger gardens. Remember, for instance, that you must be able to walk next to someone, so paths cannot be too narrow. They need to look too big, in fact, in a garden which has not yet been planted. When the plants become fully established, the paths will appear to be a lot less wide.

If you have a lot of pavement stones or shingle paving stones, you can use these for the paving. Lay them in a block system: four together with another contrasting material in between. Turn the shingle stones, so that the grey comes on top. That is restful and

Wooden bridges combine well with water areas.

127

nicer looking than the rather dated layer of shingle, which is really the decorative side of the stone. If you have elongated stones of 40 x 60cm (16 x 24in), you are left with a hole in the middle when you lay a square shape. I solved this problem in a recently laid-out garden, by inserting layers of almost black cobble-stones, which were also placed around the outside of the four stones. The square of stones is 1 x 1m (3 x 3ft) in itself, the edge usually 15cm (6in) wide.

Grey concrete cobble-stones This is a very successful new material made of concrete with a colouring agent in it. Shades of reddish-blue, browny-yellow, or light and dark grey are available. These are actually cobble-stones made of concrete, because the corners have been quite deliberately chipped away slightly. This is done by shaking the stones together. An advantage of these new concrete "cobble-stones" is that the top is flat. So you do not have the bumpy effect of the small-headed cobbles, the top of which can never be completely flat, because the quarrymen have hacked every stone separately into shape.

A patterned paving as an ornament Many pavers take great pleasure in making a real piece of ornamental paving for a change. This is a compensation for the many car parks and streets which they pave. Sometimes they create something special, such as the peacock's tail pattern of clinkers or cobbles. These are laid in a fan-shape: you begin with one cobble-stone, then

Paving should be laid on sand beds of, ideally, 15cm (6in). Once the paving has been put down, river sand is poured over it to fill in the joins. The stones here are joined at half-stone intervals; what this expert is doing here is making a round edge which goes across the lines of the circle.

128

two, then three, working up to five; at the same time you make sure
that you end up with a half arch to finish off each fan. This is a
splendid idea if you have to make large terraces which would otherwise be rather boring. Many people are mad about circular shapes,
just as I am; even in a square terrace or in a rectangle you can work
with circles. Try to make the heart of a clinker terrace with the
familiar small-headed stones and vary the direction of the paving.
I am not very fond of the combination of clinkers with cobbles
myself. It is often rather heavy, but with modest use of the cobble-
stones and a restful distribution, the effect can then actually be quite
pleasant.

**_A sophisticated
surface of
Dolomite/boulder
clay_**

Among my current favourite pavings is Dolomite, or boulder clay,
which consists of loam with cobble-stones or broken pebbles. When
it rains, the loam sinks away between the pebbles, leaving a hard,
ochre/sand-coloured layer.

It is splendid on terraces and paths which need to radiate tranquillity, and therefore is at the other extreme from terraces with ornamental paving. This is a good material under trees like plane trees,
as long as you have some fanciful chairs on it.

Gravel as paving

Now that there are materials which prevent the stones from sinking
and help to stop weeds growing between them, gravel has become a

*You can guess what
the intention is here.
The varying width of
the paths is designed
to force the walker to
look left and right
rather than straight
ahead.*

practical alternative to clinkers and cobble-stones, which is splendid to look at and not too expensive.

Nylon honeycomb mats are now available into which the gravel is poured. The mats keep the gravel together in honeycomb-shaped nylon segments, so that it does not slide around. Underneath the nylon honeycomb is a root-resistant canvas, which weeds cannot get through. If you find this too expensive, lay a fairly thin layer of gravel on broken rubble, which is shaken down and acts as a foundation layer.

A path of Dolomite, or boulder clay, has coarse-grained shingle or is like fine sand. In the Begeynhof in Hasselt boulder clay is used for the paths of the small newly equipped gardens.

Clinkers, an unrivalled paving material

As a landscape gardener I sometimes suffer from professional distortion: for instance, I can suddenly have enough of clinkers, because everyone seems to be using them. This is unjust, of course, because it is still a most wonderful material for restful, warm terrace paths and squares.

By using the same sort of clinkers in different patterns, attractive variations are created. Be careful with the combination of yellow and red clinkers; you must have a lot of restful green or grey around them if you do not want the effect to be too turbulent.

Keep the use of clinkers simple, because there are plants and items of furniture which demand attention too.

Lots of terraces

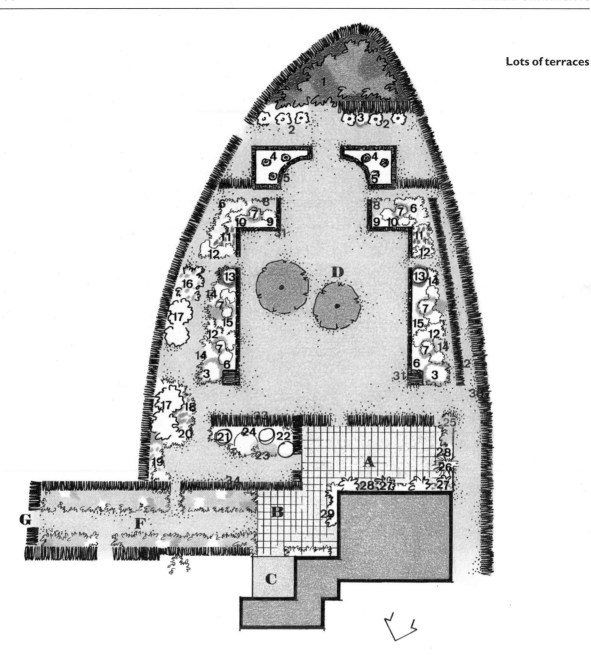

A sun terrace

B little box garden on terrace

C roofed terrace

D large lawn with two old apple trees

E private, semi-wild shady garden with
   small pond

F pink borders

G view of meadows between yew hedges

1 *Exochorda racemosa*

2 standard *Hydrangea paniculata*

3 *Rosa* 'Schneewittchen'

4 *Rosa* 'Maria Mathilda'

5 standard *Rosa* 'Schneewittchen'

6 *Cimicifuga dahurica*

7 *Rosa* 'White Fleurette'

8 *Bergenia* 'Silberschmelze'

9 *Dicentra eximia* 'Alba'

10 *Artemisia* 'Powys Castle'

11 *Anemone* 'Honorine Jobert'

12 *Anaphalis triplinervis*

13 *Helleborus corsicus*

14 *Aster cordifolius* 'Silver Spray'

15 *Chelone* 'Alba'

16 *Viburnum burkwoodii*

17 *Rhododendron* 'Cunningham's White'

18 *Lamium galeobdolon*

19 *Luzula sylvatica*

20 *Phyllitis scolopendrium*

21 *Acer palmatum* 'Dissectum'

22 *Astilbe* 'Weisse Gloria'

23 *Brunnera macrophylla*

24 *Hedera helix* 'Arborescens'

25 *Hydrangea sargentiana*

26 *Sinarundinaria murielae*

27 *Crambe cordifolia*

28 *Hedera colchica* 'Arborescens'

29 *Hydrangea paniculata*

30 hedge of *Crateagus monogyna*

31 small hedges of *Buxus sempervirens*

32 hedge of *Taxus baccata*

33 hedge of *Prunus laurocerasus*
    'Rotundifolia'

34 hedge of *Carpinus betulus*

Terraces

In the previous chapters many aspects of eating in the garden have been discussed, so I shall limit myself here to the right place for a terrace, sun and shade, and a lowered or raised position.

The right place for a terrace

Make things easy for yourself and put a pile of matching cushions somewhere near the kitchen or terrace door. Then you can sit down in white clothes without having to worry about green marks on your clothes.

I like sun, but also shade, so in a not very large garden I make a terrace in the sun with a tree which puts part of the terrace in shadow. You can do this with a light tree, such as birch, ornamental apple, true apple, acacia, or even a nut tree, which often grows so big that after many years you have to build a separate terrace somewhere else. You can have pergolas or parasols instead of a tree like this. The fact that parasols have the advantage of being portable and removable means that many people choose them. That is a pity, as a green shady spot like this is magnificent and causes no problems. In France, Italy, Spain, and Portugal you sometimes eat in courtyards or on restaurant terraces, which have iron wires stretched between walls and poles; grapevines are trained over them and this gives a pattern of marvellous light and shade.

Early in the spring and late in the autumn you look for warmth, because the air all around is cooler; if there is sunshine you can still sit outside. So a spot which takes this into account is ideal. Look for a spot not too far from the house, where the sun shines longest, and build the terrace there. If there are several places, build several terraces or go and sit on the grass, which you have sown in a second sunny spot. It is easy if you can drive a dining trolley with caterpillar tracks through the garden, with all the knives and forks and food and drink on it; in this case you must make garden paths and terraces without steps. But, on the other hand, a sunken sitting area is

In Belgium and America many terraces are laid in concrete. This means freedom from maintenance. Here layers of pots with one variety of geranium decorate the breakfast terrace.

Perennials, roses, shrubs, and trees as ornaments

There are restless garden lovers who feel an irresistible urge to keep regrouping plants in different ways.

At the entrance to Groot Buggenum Castle in Limburg, four of these lead vases stand in four corners, with the rose 'New Dawn' trained over them.

For them it is torment to have to wait until the autumn before they can change everything in the garden again. These gardeners swear by the so-called "mobile" garden, in which it is possible to make fascinating arrangements with a large number of pots, troughs, and plant containers round the terrace, by the front door, or at the bottom of the garden on a patio. Almost everyone feels the need, to a lesser or greater extent, to change something now and then, for example, if pots of annuals have just finished flowering or a bush is beginning to look very boring in its container. Then it is quite right to move the pots around. To make an attractive composition it is a good idea to put plants of different characters in pots. There are the almost indispensable box globes and the pots with lavender and thyme as evergreen emphases. You can have bushes, such as a camellia, or a maple, which grows fancifully, or perhaps roses or perennials in pots, such as *Hosta* or *Sedum*, which are almost indestructible in pots. Annuals also belong to this mobile spectacle, which can be restful or, in contrast, varied in colour.

Grey mobile planting

Elaeagnus ebbingei is a strong pot plant, which can be globe or square shaped. The leaves are elongated and silver-grey underneath and greeny-grey on the upper surface. Trim firmly and regularly throughout the growing season, as gigantic shoots appear on this plant, which has good resistance to frost, at unexpected moments and places. *Pyrus salicifolia* and *Elaeagnus angustifolia*, which are both a beautiful silver-grey, are not evergreen. They are loose-growing bushes, which are popular because of their fancifulness, and move in the wind like elegant parasols above the pots of shorter plants. They are dependable grey bushes.

There are also grey perennials: lavender, *Stachys* (elephant's ear), *Helichrysum* (straw flowers), *Santolina*, *Ruta* (rue), etc. *Hosta* also has varieties with blue-grey leaf colouring, which do well in pots. There are also grey annuals, such as *Ballota*.

Colour variations

A gold variegated group

Put a brightly coloured *Aucuba japonica* 'Variegata' in a sturdy container, and plant a gold variegated elder, maple, or *Cornus* with it. Complete the picture with gold variegated sage and gold variegated comfrey.

Next to these have pots of yellow slipperwort (*Calceolaria*), yellow perennial violets, and yellow *Sedum kamtschaticum*, which is also perennial and remains short.

White variegated

The pretty, white-striped strawberry is growing in my garden. I do not know yet whether it has fruit; I think it does. Silver variegated thyme, like silver variegated sage, silver variegated phlox and many of the silvery *Artemisias*, is not flecked, but uniformly silver-coloured. Combine these with blue colours, such as heliotrope, dark and light

Beech begins slowly, but once this giant tree has grown in its bonsai form into a hedge, a thick green wall can be made out of it, which can act as a good background for statues, benches, or garden vases.

blue *Petunia*, and dark blue *Lobelia*. Simple green can also be fascinating, as long as it is varied.

Green tints   If you take notice of plants, you will know that there are great differences in leaf forms, in the delicacy of distribution, and in size. If you consider this when making a green composition, it need not be boring, but can be quite fascinating.

The fine greenery of southernwood contrasts with angelica, which has broad veined leaves. Fine-leafed hyssop contrasts with coarse-leafed valerian: one has blue flowers and the other pink. *Catalpa* as a bush is good in a container, as are all kinds of laurel varieties, such as *Prunus laurocerasus* and the *Prunus lusitanica*. *Aucuba* is another evergreen bush which loves being in a pot and produces long coarse leaves.

Rhododendron likes a pot which is kept well watered. A fine-leafed bush like contorted acacia (*Robinia pseudoacacia* 'Tortuosa') is attractive with its fine foliage, and so is ornamental willow. To give height there are again the large green leaves of *Hosta undulata* and those of the large butterbur (*Petasites*), which also thrives well in a pot, as long as it always has a saucer of water underneath it.

As an annual there is *Nicotiana*, which has coarse foliage, while cosmea (*Cosmos*) has fine foliage; *Lobelia* is fine-leafed and *Canna*, the tuber which grows to a height of 2m (6ft), is very coarse-leafed.

Most ornamental grasses remain interesting, certainly in the autumn and well into the winter, with their browny-yellow tints, which eventually fade and decompose.

A pond as an ornament

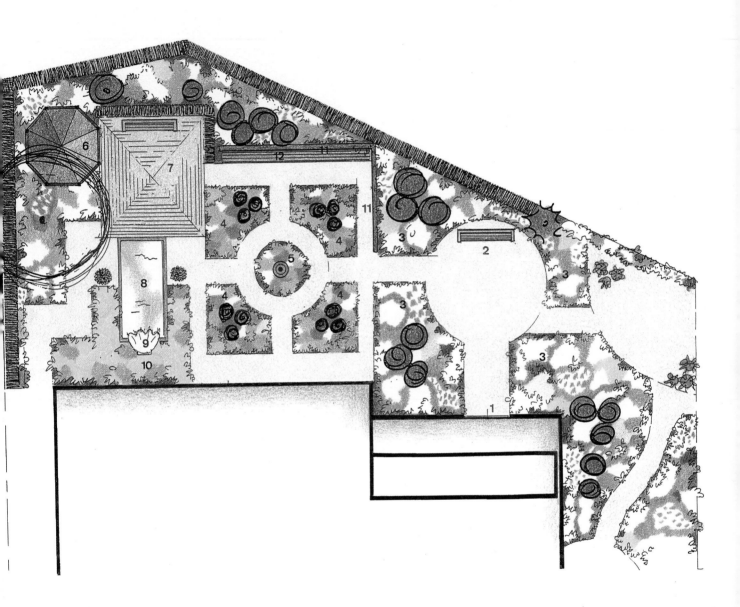

1 conservatory

2 Lutyens bench with lead pots

3 white planting with roses, *Astrantia*,
  Crambe cordifolia

4 low blue garden with lavender, *Nepeta*,
  and *Campanula portenschlagiana*

5 ornament: a lead globe

6 mauve-blue painted summer-house

7 brick terrace

8 stone edge around concrete pond

9 shell-shaped water tank

10 bamboo and lots of large foliage plants
   and hortensias

11 mauve-blue trelliswork for blue
   Clematis

12 site for a small bench without back, grey

Sound in the garden

You can discover the function and charm of fountains and spouts in countries such as Spain, Italy, Turkey, and Portugal. I saw these at their most remarkable at a cathedral and pilgrimage site near Lisbon. The cathedral stands high up, at the top of a flight of steps.

This flight of steps is part of the journey that the pilgrim undertakes to beg a favour of God. You really ought to climb these steps on your knees, but you can also try walking up. It is not a long straight flight of steps going upwards, which would certainly mean a climb of 5–6m (16–20ft). There are always two flights of steps which start with some flat steps. One goes left, the other right, and then they change direction half way in a zigzag shape, so that you come out at some more flat steps with two more flights of steps. Each set of steps has a fountain, which has been carved out of the side of the mountain. Part of the head of the fountain on each set of steps is used as a water-spouting feature. One set of steps has a head, from which water spouts from the eyes. People come here if they have trouble with their eyes. On the following steps water comes out of the nose, then out of the ears, then out of the mouth. All the faces are quite primitive, but for this reason quite "authentically" carved.

In the gardens of the Vatican there are stone children which spout water. In the private section of the Pope's large gardens there is a flat garden, situated high up, with iron arches, over which sweet-smelling climbing jasmine has been trained. Cupids stand here in round basins and are sprayed with water, so that their bodies shine.

Spouting frogs Rosemary Verey is one of the best-known English authors of gardening books at the moment. Together with her husband, Charles, a

Water spouts fixed high up on walls are a real find. I do this with freestone chutes. Here it is successfully achieved with a lead ornament, from which water flows into the basin placed beneath.

famous restoration architect, she moved into the ancestral home, which is built in "William and Mary" style: simple, stylish architecture, owing to the symmetry which can be seen everywhere. Symmetrical forms can be found in the garden too. For instance, there are two little avenues situated next to each other, which have been laid as cross-axes opposite the main axis, which stands at right angles to the rear elevation. One of them is bordered by lime trees, which have been trimmed into standard hedges. The other is formed from a series of arches, round which *Wisteria* and *Laburnum* (golden rain tree) have been planted. This gives an attractive variation in colour. As under-planting there are red tulips, by which I mean 'Apeldoorn', which are thrillingly rich in colour with the yellow of the laburnum.

Then follow the globe onions, which are just as thrilling, because they stand more or less in the half-shadow and grow enormous, to produce a sea of purple globes. At the end of this green spectacle is a basin. This basin is a pond, with flagstones round it, between which some little creepers can grow. Behind the basin an old garden wall is only half visible, because there is a sculpture in front of it. It is a large rectangular block of sandstone, which has rams' heads on the sides. The heads have moss growing on them, which is partly caused by two fat stone frogs, which sit on the ground and spout water at the middle of the stone block. Around and behind the frogs are *Hosta* and *Polygonum*. The atmosphere is moist and rather wild.

Hosta sieboldiana 'Elegans' and many other shade-loving plants grow around the water spout.

139

In this way all sorts of things are brought together to create a sight-line: the arches, a subtle spectacle created by the carved block, and the moss-covered frogs.

Little chutes in a modern garden

I once designed a modern garden, which had fairly radical consequences for the existing situation. There were many fruit trees in the back garden, which were crying out for the pruning knife: nuts, rowan trees, and birches. The garden was a shady forest, just right for hammocks and swings; therefore ideal for children. Then came my plan, in which I further developed the lines of the house to bring structure and sun into the whole garden with terraces, walls, and plant containers. A large straight pond, which I drew as a sight axis, became a swimming pool, and the result was that all the fruit trees, birches, and a number of rowan trees disappeared.

Iron ornamental vases are on sale everywhere; put something together with them and create out of them a gurgling eye-catcher, as in this old Italian garden.

To keep some suspense in the garden, though, I extended the walls of the house on the right and the left, so that walled terraces were created on both sides, which offered maximum privacy. The slightly sunken swimming pool lay beside the long left-hand wall, next to the terrace. A pergola with reinforced glass acts as a roof to this terrace with its round cane furniture. The right-hand terrace is partly enclosed by the wall, which forms a corner. A rectangular pond closes off this terrace on one side. Or so it seems: stepping stones have been laid across the pond, so that you can escape. Wall and pond link up with each other. Stone chutes have been installed there, which have been put quite high up, so that you can hear the lively sound of falling water. In practice, however, stone chutes are not without their problems. Water, which comes out of a pipe and is carried further by a stone chute like this, trickles back along the bottom of the chute, and the wall underneath becomes damp. In this garden the walls were painted pale yellow-ochre, which had the disadvantage that the painted walls went greenish under the stream of water.

Jets of water from lions' heads

There are firms which reproduce all sorts of old ornaments. They often choose famous ornaments from private collections. The material used is a mixture of sandstone chippings and cold cement. It is pressed into moulds, until the whole thing becomes very hard in the mould. There are water spouts ranging from little boys with a dolphin in their arms spouting water, to lions' heads, which are fixed to a wall and spout water from their mouths. These are old Italian ornaments, which can be seen in bronze all over Italy, which has so much garden ornamentation.

In a long, thin back garden plastered walls had been built on the left and the right, and these lions' heads had been mounted on them on both sides. They were massive heads, which had been brought home after being carefully packed abroad. But they had not been packed carefully enough, because the nose of one and the chin of another was damaged. It would be better to buy in your own country,

Facing page: Stone walls are often slightly porous, or are of a structure which means that water dripping on to them leads to the growth of algae and ferns and other vegetative embellishment.

possibly in a bronze version which would probably be more suitable for an ordinary garden.

Fountains, birds and games with the wind

Birds eat insects, such as lice and caterpillars and snails and are therefore worth enticing into our gardens. This can be done, among other ways, by providing water for them to drink, and in which they can bathe. For this reason a low edge around the water container must be made, which can be of wood, stone, or peat, although the latter can be problematical, for instance if you have a lot of pigeons which return regularly. The peat can suffer in time, and chicken wire has to be put over it, in the place where the planting is lowest and the birds usually come to drink. If you want to let them bathe, a bowl of water which is regularly refilled and cleaned, is the best thing. A bathing spot like this must be shallow, otherwise they will drown.

In my garden in Zeeland I have had a pit dug; a pond has been put in here which serves as a drinking place for the above-mentioned birds. It is natural water with a gently sloping side, so that the sheep standing on one side of it do not drown. The other side is my ornamental garden. Gates close them both off at the sides. It is a treat to see how all the birds in the neighbourhood come and bathe on this gentle slope. This is an idea then if you are making a pond: make the side which you look at most very gently sloping. Then the birds will arrive of their own accord. To keep the water clear and for the fish

This pink marble water container is decorated with a pair of ornaments: a little head, out of which water flows, and above it a splendid cupid.

Left: In Haastrecht I designed a water ornament which is needed to drown out the sound of neighbouring traffic. A Gothic sandstone spout and trellis were designed and a semicircular brick pond and pump were installed in front of an old brick wall.

A simple fountain works miracles in a pond for the production of oxygen and sound, which is usually regarded as pleasantly distracting and peaceful.

which will possibly be put into it, it is important to add oxygen. You can do this with the waterspouts already described, or it can be done with a simple fountain. I prefer fountains which spout straight upwards. With stalks of reed mace around them they make a splendid picture, and the splashing can drown out an annoying noise elsewhere.

You can try to use an old lesson from landscape gardening. Imagine a long pond, which is situated so that you look over the top of it. If the water surface is completely flat, it has the effect of a large flat mirror, in which the clouds or the cloudless blue sky are reflected. This is why children always depict water as blue. In reality it is not always so: just fill a bottle or a bucket with pond water: you will see anything but blue.

If you like perspective with ponds, you can try to do the same as they do with large ponds in parks. Taller plants are deliberately planted in groups along the edge and other parts are kept low or not planted, so that the wind blows across the low planted area. You then get lines of wind on the water, which starts to "glitter". I once saw this in Kensington Park in London, where the enormous length of the pond was given suspense, by quite intentionally using these lines of wind on the water next to areas which were completely smooth and protected from the wind by tall spinneys. So there is a lot to learn and to discover for oneself, just by taking a simple walk in a wood, park, or garden, which may have important consequences for the

In the formal pond garden of Groot Buggenum Castle, a stone vase has been placed centrally in the pond water. Water often flows out of it, so oxygen enters the water of the pond.

Photo credits

A. J. van der Horst, Amsterdam: title page, pp. 6, 8, 9, 10, 12, 14, 16, 17, 18, 19, 20, 22, 27, 28, 29, 30, 34, 37, 39, 40, 41, 43, 44, 45, 47, 50, 52, 53, 54, 55, 58 left, 62, 63, 64, 65, 66, 76 right, 83, 84 left, 85 bottom, 86, 87, 88, 90 to 99 inclusive, 104, 105, 111, 113, 114, 115, 118, 119, 120, 121, 122 left, 123, 124, 130, 132 right, 138 left, 139, 140, 142 right, 143 bottom

M. Kurpershoek, Amsterdam: pp. 13, 23, 24, 25, 36, 56, 57, 58 right, 59, 61, 69, 73, 76 left, 77, 81, 85 top, 89, 100, 101, 102, 110 top, 112, 117, 125, 126, 127, 128, 129, 132 top left, 136 left

G. Otter, IJsselstein: pp. 7, 15 bottom, 31, 38, 51, 67, 68, 71, 72, 74, 78, 79, 82, 84 right, 103, 106, 107, 108, 109, 116, 122 right, 133, 141

The author thanks Rianne van Bergen, Amsterdam, for her indispensable help in the realization of this book.